# Using OpenRefine

The essential OpenRefine guide that takes you from data analysis and error fixing to linking your dataset to the Web

**Ruben Verborgh**

**Max De Wilde**

BIRMINGHAM - MUMBAI

# Using OpenRefine

First published: September 2013

Production Reference: 1040913

Published by Packt Publishing Ltd.
Livery Place
35 Livery Street
Birmingham B3 2PB, UK.

ISBN 978-1-78328-908-0

www.packtpub.com

Cover Image by Aniket Sawant (aniket_sawant_photography@hotmail.com)

# Credits

**Authors**
Ruben Verborgh
Max De Wilde

**Reviewers**
Martin Magdinier
Dr. Mateja Verlic

**Acquisition Editor**
Sam Birch

**Commissioning Editor**
Subho Gupta

**Technical Editors**
Anita Nayak
Harshad Vairat

**Project Coordinator**
Sherin Padayatty

**Proofreader**
Paul Hindle

**Indexer**
Hemangini Bari

**Production Coordinator**
Nilesh R. Mohite

**Cover Work**
Nilesh R. Mohite

# Foreword

At the time I joined Metaweb Technologies, Inc. in 2008, we were building up Freebase in earnest; entity by entity, fact by fact. Now you may know Freebase through its newest incarnation, Google's Knowledge Graph, which powers the "Knowledge panels" on www.google.com.

Building up "the world's database of everything" is a tall order that machines and algorithms alone cannot do, even if raw public domain data exists in abundance. Raw data from multiple sources must be cleaned up, homogenized, and then reconciled with data already in Freebase. Even that first step of cleaning up the data cannot be automated entirely; it takes the common sense of a human reader to know that if both 0.1 and 10,000,000 occur in a column named cost, they are very likely in different units (perhaps millions of dollars and dollars respectively). It also takes a human reader to decide that UCBerkley means the same as University of California in Berkeley, CA, but not the same as Berkeley DB.

If these errors occur often enough, we might as well have given up or just hired enough people to perform manual data entry. But these errors occur often enough to be a problem, and yet not often enough that anyone who has not dealt with such data thinks simple automation is sufficient. But, dear reader, you have dealt with data, and you know how unpredictably messy it can be.

Every dataset that we wanted to load into Freebase became an iterative exercise in programming mixed with manual inspection that led to hard-coding transformation rules, from turning two-digit years into four-digits, to swapping given name and surname if there is a comma in between them. Even for most of us programmers, this exercise got old quickly, and it was painful to start every time.

So, we created Freebase Gridworks, a tool for cleaning up data and making it ready for loading into Freebase. We designed it to be a database-spreadsheet hybrid; it is interactive like spreadsheet software and programmable like databases. It was this combination that made Gridworks the first of its kind.

In the process of creating and then using Gridworks ourselves, we realized that cleaning, transforming, and just playing with data is crucial and generally useful, even if the goal is not to load data into Freebase. So, we redesigned the tool to be more generic, and released its Version 2 under the name "Google Refine" after Google acquired Metaweb.

Since then, Refine has been well received in many different communities; data journalists, open data enthusiasts, librarians, archivists, hacktivists, and even programmers and developers by trade. Its adoption in the early days spread through word of mouth, in hackathons and informal tutorials held by its own users.

Having proven itself through early adopters, Refine now needs better organized efforts to spread and become a mature product with a sustainable community around it. Expert users, open source contributors, and data enthusiast groups are actively teaching how to use Refine on tours and in the classroom. Ruben and Max from the Free Your Metadata team have taken the next logical step in consolidating those tutorials and organizing those recipes into this handy missing manual for Refine.

Stepping back to take in the bigger picture, we may realize that messy data is not anyone's own problem, but it is more akin to ensuring that one's neighborhood is safe and clean. It is not a big problem, but it has implications on big issues such as transparency in government. Messy data discourages analysis and hides real-world problems, and we all have to roll up our sleeves to do the cleaning.

**David Huynh**
Original creator of OpenRefine

# About the Authors

**Ruben Verborgh** is a PhD researcher in Semantic Hypermedia. He is fascinated by the Web's immense possibilities and tries to contribute ideas that will maybe someday slightly influence the way the Web changes all of us. His degree in Computer Science Engineering convinced him more than ever that communication is the most crucial thing for IT-based solutions. This is why he really enjoys explaining things to those eager to learn. In 2011, he launched the Free Your Metadata project together with Seth van Hooland and Max De Wilde, which aims to evangelize the importance of bringing your data on the Web. This book is one of the assets in this continuing quest.

He currently works at Multimedia Lab, a research group of iMinds, Ghent University, Belgium, in the domains of Semantic Web, Web APIs, and Adaptive Hypermedia. Together with Seth van Hooland, he's writing *Linked Data for Libraries, Archives, and Museums, Facet Publishing*, a practical guide for metadata practitioners.

**Max De Wilde** is a PhD researcher in Natural Language Processing and a teaching assistant at the Université libre de Bruxelles (ULB), department of Information and Communication Sciences. He holds a Master's degree in Linguistics from the ULB and an Advanced Master's in Computational Linguistics from the University of Antwerp. Currently, he is preparing a doctoral thesis on the impact of language-independent information extraction on document retrieval. At the same time, he works as a full-time assistant and supervises practical classes for Master's level students in a number of topics, including database quality, document management, and architecture of information systems.

# About the Reviewers

**Martin Magdinier**, during the last six years, has been heavily engaged with startup and open data communities in France, Vietnam, and Canada. Through his recent projects (TTCPass and Objectif Neige) and consulting positions, he became intimate with data massage techniques. Coming from a business approach, his focus is on data management and transformation tools that empower the business user. In 2011, he started to blog tips and tutorials on OpenRefine to help other business users to make the most out of this tool. In 2012, when Google released the software to the community, he helped to structure the new organization. Today, he continues to actively support the OpenRefine user base and advocates its usage in various communities.

**Dr. Mateja Verlic** is Head of Research at Zemanta and is an enthusiastic developer of the LOD-friendly distribution of OpenRefine. After finishing her PhD in Computer Science, she worked for two years as Assistant Professor at the University of Maribor, focusing mostly on machine learning, intelligent systems, text mining, and sentiment analysis. In 2011, when she joined Zemanta as an urban ninja and researcher, she began exploring the semantic web and has been really passionate about web technologies, lean startup, community projects, and open source software ever since.

# www.PacktPub.com

## Support files, eBooks, discount offers and more

You might want to visit www.PacktPub.com to download the datasets and projects to follow along with the recipes in this book.

Did you know that Packt offers eBook versions of every book published, with PDF and ePub files available? You can upgrade to the eBook version at www.PacktPub.com and as a print book customer, you are entitled to a discount on the eBook copy. Get in touch with us at service@packtpub.com for more details.

At www.PacktPub.com, you can also read a collection of free technical articles, sign up for a range of free newsletters and receive exclusive discounts and offers on Packt books and eBooks.

http://PacktLib.PacktPub.com

Do you need instant solutions to your IT questions? PacktLib is Packt's online digital book library. Here, you can access, read and search across Packt's entire library of books.

## Why Subscribe?

- Fully searchable across every book published by Packt
- Copy and paste, print and bookmark content
- On demand and accessible via web browser

## Free Access for Packt account holders

If you have an account with Packt at www.PacktPub.com, you can use this to access PacktLib today and view nine entirely free books. Simply use your login credentials for immediate access.

*To Linda, for her ever-lasting and loving support*

*Ruben Verborgh*

*To Hélène, and baby Jeanne*

*Max De Wilde*

# Table of Contents

# Preface

Data is often dubbed the new gold, as it is of tremendous value for today's data-driven economy. However, we prefer to think of data as diamonds.
At first they're raw, but through great skills, they can be polished to become the shiny assets that are so worthy to us. This is precisely what this book covers; how your dataset can be transformed in OpenRefine so you can optimize its quality for real-world (re)use.

As the vast amount of functionality of OpenRefine can be overwhelming to new users, we are convinced that a decent manual can make the difference. This book will guide you from your very first steps to really advanced operations that you probably didn't know were possible. We will spend time on all different aspects of OpenRefine, so in the end, you will have obtained the necessary skills to revive your own datasets. This book starts out with cleaning the data to fix small errors, and ends by linking your dataset to others so it can become part of a larger data ecosystem.

We realize that every dataset is different, yet learning is easiest by example.
This is why we have chosen the Powerhouse Museum dataset to demonstrate the techniques in this book. However, since not all steps apply on your dataset, we have structured the different tasks as recipes. Just like in a regular cookbook, you can just pick the recipes you need for what you want to achieve. Some recipes depend on each other, but this is indicated at the start of each chapter.

In addition, the example dataset in this book illustrates a healthy data culture; the people at Powerhouse decided to bring it online even though they were aware that there were still some quality issues. Interestingly, that didn't stop them from doing it, and in fact, it shouldn't stop you; the important thing is to get the data out. Since then, the data quality has significantly improved, but we're providing you with the old version so you can perform the cleaning and linking yourself.

We are confident this book will explain all the tools necessary to help you get your data in the best possible shape. As soon as you master the skill of polishing, the raw data diamonds you have right now will become shiny diamonds.

Have fun learning OpenRefine!

Ruben and Max.

# What this book covers

*Chapter 1, Diving Into OpenRefine*, teaches you the basic steps of OpenRefine, showing you how to import a dataset and how to get around in the main interface.

*Chapter 2, Analyzing and Fixing Data*, explains how you can get to know your dataset and how to spot errors in it. In addition, you'll also learn several techniques to repair mistakes.

*Chapter 3, Advanced Data Operations*, dives deeper into dataset repair, demonstrating some of the more sophisticated data operations OpenRefine has to offer.

*Chapter 4, Linking Datasets*, connects your dataset to others through reconciliation of single terms and with named-entity recognition on full-text fields.

*Appendix, Regular Expressions and GREL*, introduces you to advanced pattern matching and the General Refine Expression Language.

# What you need for this book

This book does not assume any prior knowledge; we'll even guide you through the installation of OpenRefine in *Chapter 1, Diving Into OpenRefine*.

# Who this book is for

This book is for anybody who is working with data, particularly large datasets. If you've been wondering how you can gain an insight into the issues within your data, increase its quality, or link it to other datasets, then this book is for you.

No prior knowledge of OpenRefine is assumed, but if you've worked with OpenRefine before, you'll still be able to learn new things in this book. We cover several advanced techniques in the later chapters, with *Chapter 4, Linking Datasets*, entirely devoted to linking your dataset.

# Conventions

In this book, you will find a number of styles of text that distinguish between different kinds of information. Here are some examples of these styles, and an explanation of their meaning.

Program code inside text is shown as follows: "The expression that transforms the reconciled cell to its URL is `cell.recon.match.id`".

**New terms** are shown in bold. Words that you see on the screen, in menus or dialog boxes for example, appear in the text like this: "After clicking on **OK**, you will see a new column with the corresponding URLs".

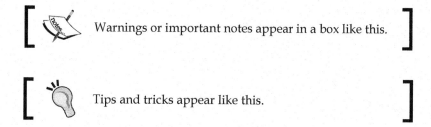

> Warnings or important notes appear in a box like this.

> Tips and tricks appear like this.

# Reader feedback

Feedback from our readers is always welcome. Let us know what you think about this book—what you liked or may have disliked. Reader feedback is important for us to develop titles that you really get the most out of.

To send us general feedback, simply send an e-mail to `feedback@packtpub.com`, and mention the book title via the subject of your message.

If there is a topic that you have expertise in and you are interested in either writing or contributing to a book, see our author guide on `www.packtpub.com/authors`.

# Customer support

Now that you are the proud owner of a Packt book, we have a number of things to help you to get the most from your purchase.

# Downloading the example files

You can download the raw data and OpenRefine projects to follow along with the recipes in the book. Each chapter has its own example file which can be downloaded from your account at `http://www.packtpub.com`. If you purchased this book elsewhere, you can visit `http://www.packtpub.com/support` and register to have the files e-mailed directly to you.

# Errata

Although we have taken every care to ensure the accuracy of our content, mistakes do happen. If you find a mistake in one of our books—maybe a mistake in the text or the code—we would be grateful if you would report this to us. By doing so, you can save other readers from frustration and help us improve subsequent versions of this book. If you find any errata, please report them by visiting `http://www.packtpub.com/submit-errata`, selecting your book, clicking on the **errata submission form** link, and entering the details of your errata. Once your errata are verified, your submission will be accepted and the errata will be uploaded on our website, or added to any list of existing errata, under the Errata section of that title. Any existing errata can be viewed by selecting your title from `http://www.packtpub.com/support`.

# Piracy

Piracy of copyright material on the Internet is an ongoing problem across all media. At Packt, we take the protection of our copyright and licenses very seriously. If you come across any illegal copies of our works, in any form, on the Internet, please provide us with the location address or website name immediately so that we can pursue a remedy.

Please contact us at `copyright@packtpub.com` with a link to the suspected pirated material.

We appreciate your help in protecting our authors, and our ability to bring you valuable content.

# Questions

You can contact us at `questions@packtpub.com` if you are having a problem with any aspect of the book, and we will do our best to address it.

# 1
# Diving Into OpenRefine

In this opening chapter, we will discover what OpenRefine is made for, why you should use it, and how. After a short introduction, we will go through seven fundamental recipes that will give you a foretaste of the power of OpenRefine:

- Recipe 1 – installing OpenRefine
- Recipe 2 – creating a new project
- Recipe 3 – exploring your data
- Recipe 4 – manipulating columns
- Recipe 5 – using the project history
- Recipe 6 – exporting a project
- Recipe 7 – going for more memory

Although every recipe can be read independently from the others, we recommend that readers who are new to OpenRefine stick to the original order, at least for the first few recipes, since they provide crucial information about its general workings. More advanced users who already have an OpenRefine installation running can pick our tricks in any order they like.

## Introducing OpenRefine

Let's face a hard fact: your data are messy. All data are messy. Errors will always creep into large datasets no matter how much care you have put into creating them, especially when their creation has involved several persons and/or has been spread over a long timespan. Whether your data are born-digital or have been digitized, whether they are stored in a spreadsheet or in a database, something will always go awry somewhere in your dataset.

Acknowledging this messiness is the first essential step towards a sensible approach to data quality, which mainly involves data profiling and cleaning.

**Data profiling** is defined by Olson (*Data Quality: The Accuracy Dimension, Jack E. Olson, Morgan Kaufman, 2003*) as "the use of analytical techniques to discover the true structure, content, and quality of data". In other words, it is a way to get an assessment of the current state of your data and information about errors that they contain.

**Data cleaning** is the process that tries to correct those errors in a semi-automated way by removing blanks and duplicates, filtering and faceting rows, clustering and transforming values, splitting multi-valued cells, and so on.

Whereas custom scripts were formerly needed to perform data profiling and cleaning tasks, often separately, the advent of **Interactive Data Transformation tools (IDTs)** now allows for quick and inexpensive operations on large amounts of data inside a single integrated interface, even by domain professionals lacking in-depth technical skills.

OpenRefine is such an IDT; a tool for visualizing and manipulating data. It looks like a traditional, Excel-like spreadsheet software, but it works rather like a database, that is, with columns and fields rather than individual cells. This means that OpenRefine is not well suited for encoding new rows of data, but is extremely powerful when it comes to exploring, cleaning, and linking data.

The recipes gathered in this first chapter will help you to get acquainted with OpenRefine by reviewing its main functionalities, from import/export to data exploration and from history usage to memory management.

# Recipe 1 – installing OpenRefine

In this recipe, you will learn where to look in order to **download** the latest release of OpenRefine and how to **get it running** on your favorite operating system.

First things first: start by downloading OpenRefine from `http://openrefine.org/`. OpenRefine was previously known as Freebase Gridworks, then as Google Refine for a few years. Since October 2012, the project has been taken over by the community, which makes OpenRefine really open. OpenRefine 2.6 is the first version carrying the new branding. If you are interested in the development version, you can also check `https://github.com/OpenRefine`.

OpenRefine is based on the Java environment, which makes it platform-independent. Just make sure that you have an up-to-date version of Java running on your machine (available from `http://java.com/download`) and follow the following instructions, depending on your operating system:

# Windows

1.  Download the ZIP archive.

2.  Unzip and extract the contents of the archive to a folder of your choice.

3.  To launch OpenRefine, double-click on `openrefine.exe`.

# Mac

1.  Download the DMG file.

2.  Open the disk image and drag the OpenRefine icon into the `Applications` folder.

3.  Double-click on the icon to start OpenRefine.

# Linux

1.  Download the gzipped tarball.

2.  Extract the folder to your home directory.

3.  In a terminal, enter `./refine` to start.

It should be noted that, by default, OpenRefine will allocate only 1 GB of RAM to Java. While this is sufficient to handle small datasets, it soon becomes restrictive when dealing with larger collections of data. In *Recipe 7 – going for more memory*, we will detail how to allow OpenRefine to allocate more memory, an operation that also differs from one OS to the other.

# Recipe 2 – creating a new project

In this recipe, you will learn how to get data into OpenRefine, whether by **creating** a new project and loading a dataset, **opening** an existing project from a previous session, or **importing** someone else's project.

If you successfully installed OpenRefine and launched it as explained in *Recipe 1 – installing OpenRefine*, you will notice that OpenRefine opens in your default browser. However, it is important to realize that the application is run locally: you do not need an Internet connection to use OpenRefine, except if you want to reconcile your data with external sources through the use of extensions (see *Appendix, Regular Expressions and GREL* for such advanced uses). Be also reassured that your sensitive data will not be stored online or shared with anyone. In practice, OpenRefine uses the port 3333 of your local machine, which means that it will be available through the URL `http://localhost:3333/` or `http://127.0.0.1:3333/`.

Here is the start screen you will be looking at when you first open OpenRefine:

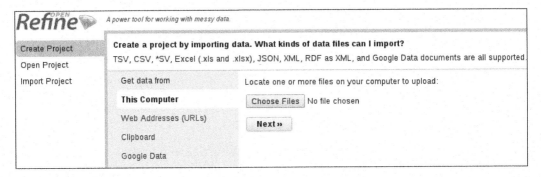

On the left, three tabs are available:

- **Create Project**: This option loads a dataset into OpenRefine. This is what you will want when you use OpenRefine for the first time. There are various supported formats, as shown in the preceding screenshot. You can import data in different ways:
  - **This Computer**: Select a file stored on your local machine
  - **Web Addresses (URLs)**: Import data directly from an online source*
  - **Clipboard**: Copy-paste your data into a text field
  - **Google Data**: Enable access to a Google Spreadsheet or Fusion Table*

  *Internet connection required

- **Open Project**: This option helps you go back to an existing project created during a former session. The next time you start OpenRefine, it will show a list of existing projects and propose you to continue working on a dataset that you have been using previously.

- **Import Project**: With this option, we can directly import an existing OpenRefine project archive. This allows you to open a project that someone else has exported, including the history of all transformations already performed on the data since the project was created.

# File formats supported by OpenRefine

Here are some of the file formats supported by OpenRefine:

- Comma-Separated Values (CSV), Tab-Separated Values (TSV), and other *SV
- MS Excel documents (both .XLS and .XLSX) and Open Document Format (ODF) spreadsheets (.ODS), although the latter is not explicitly mentioned
- JavaScript Object Notation (JSON)

- XML and Resource Description Framework (RDF) as XML
- Line-based formats (logs)

If you need other formats, you can add them by way of OpenRefine extensions.

Project creation with OpenRefine is straightforward and consists of three simple steps: selecting your file , previewing the import, and validating to let OpenRefine create your project. Let's create a new project by clicking on the **Choose Files** button from the **This Computer** tab, selecting your dataset (refer to the following information box), then clicking on **Next**.

 Although we encourage you to experiment with OpenRefine on your own dataset, it may be useful for you to be able to reproduce the examples used throughout this book. In order to facilitate this, all recipes are performed on the dataset from the Powerhouse Museum in Sydney, freely available from your account at http://www.packtpub.com (use the file chapter1.tsv). Feel free to download this file and load it into OpenRefine in order to follow the recipes more easily. Files are also present for the remaining chapters in a similar format for download. If you purchased this book elsewhere, you can visit http://www.packtpub.com/support and register to have the files e-mailed directly to you.

On the next screen, you get an overview of your dataset as it will appear in OpenRefine. In the bottom-right corner, you can see the following parsing options as shown in the following screenshot:

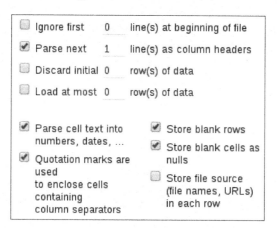

By default, the first line will be parsed as column headers, which is a common practice and relevant in the case of the Powerhouse dataset. OpenRefine will also attempt a guess for each cell type in order to differentiate text strings from integers, dates, and URLs among others. This will prove useful later when sorting your data (if you choose to keep the cells in plain text format, 10 will come before 2, for instance).

Another option demanding attention is the **Quotation marks are used to enclose cells containing column separators** checkbox. If you leave it selected, be sure to verify that the cell values are indeed enclosed in quotes in the original file. Otherwise, deselect this box to ensure that the quotation marks are not misinterpreted by OpenRefine. In the case of the Powerhouse collection, quotes are used inside cells to indicate object titles and inscriptions, for instance, so they have no syntactic meaning: we need to deselect the checkbox before going further. The other options may come in handy in some cases; try to select and deselect them in order to see how they affect your data. Also, be sure to select the right encoding to avoid special characters to being mixed up. When everything seems right, click on **Create Project** to load your data into OpenRefine.

# Recipe 3 – exploring your data

In this recipe, you will get to know your data by scanning the different **zones** giving access to the total number of **rows/records**, the various display options, the column **headers and menus**, and the actual cell contents.

Once your dataset has been loaded, you will access the main interface of OpenRefine as shown in the following screenshot:

| | | | | | |
|---|---|---|---|---|---|
| **1 75814 rows** | | | | | |
| 2 Show as: **rows** records      Show: 5 **10** 25 50 rows | | | | | |
| 3 ▼ **All** | ▼ **Record ID** | ▼ **Object Title** | ▼ **Registration Nu** | ▼ **Description.** | ▼ **Marks** |
| 4 ☆ 🗊 1. | 267220 | Rocket motor on loan from Roswell Museum and Art Center, USA | L2106-3/1 | Rocket motor, liquid fuelled combustion chamber, steel / aluminium wrapped tubes with insulation, included in flight of Dec 26 1928, Robert H Goddard, USA, 1928 (Roswell Acc No: 1958-28-12) | |
| ☆ 🗊 2. | 346260 | Fragment of moon rock on loan from National Aeronautics and Space Administration (NASA), USA | L4115/1 | Fragment of lunar sample (moon rock), NASA No.61016.116 (011) and box, weight of rock 89 grams, collected by Apollo 16 | |

Four zones are seen on this screen; let's go through them from top to bottom, numbered as 1 to 4 in the preceding screenshot:

1. **Total number of rows**: If you did not forget to specify that quotation marks are to be ignored (see *Recipe 2 – creating a new project*), you should see a total of **75814 rows** from the Powerhouse file. When data are filtered on a given criterion, this bar will display something like **123 matching rows (75814 total)**.

2. **Display options**: Try to alternate between **rows** and **records** by clicking on either word. True, not much will change, except that you may now read **75814 records** in zone 1. The number of rows is always equal to the number of records in a new project, but they will evolve independently from now on. This zone will also let you choose whether to display 5, 10, 25, or 50 rows/records on a page, and it also provides the right way to navigate from page to page.

3. **Column headers and menus**: You will find here the first row that was parsed as column headers when the project was created. In the Powerhouse dataset, the columns read **Record ID, Object Title, Registration Number**, and so on (if you deselected the **Parse next 1 line as column headers** option box, you will see **Column 1, Column 2**, and so on instead). The leftmost column is always called **All** and is divided in three subcolumns containing stars (to mark good records, for instance), flags (to mark bad records, for instance), and IDs. Starred and flagged rows can easily be faceted, as we will see in *Chapter 2, Analyzing and Fixing Data*. Every column also has a menu (see the following screenshot) that can be accessed by clicking on the small dropdown to the left of the column header.

4. **Cell contents**: This option shows the main area displaying the actual values of the cells.

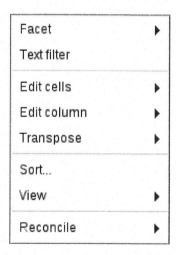

Before starting to profile and clean your data, it is important to get to know them well and to be at ease with OpenRefine: have a look at each column (using the horizontal scrollbar) to verify that the column headers have been parsed correctly, that the cell types were rightly guessed, and so on. Change the number of rows displayed per page to 50 and go through a few pages to check that the values are consistent (ideally, you should already have done so during preview before creating your project). When you feel that you are sufficiently familiar with the interface, you can consider moving along to the next recipe.

# Recipe 4 – manipulating columns

In this recipe, you will learn how the columns in OpenRefine can be **collapsed** and **expanded** again, **moved** around in any direction, or **renamed** and **removed** at leisure.

Columns are an essential part of OpenRefine: they contain thousands of values of the same nature and can be manipulated in a number of ways.

## Collapsing and expanding columns

By default, all columns are expanded in OpenRefine, which can be cumbersome if there are many in the project. If you want to temporarily hide one or more columns to facilitate the work on the others, click on the dropdown in any column to show the menu and select **View**. Four options are available to you:

- Collapse this column
- Collapse all other columns
- Collapse columns to left
- Collapse columns to right

Here is a screenshot of the Powerhouse dataset after navigating to **View | Collapse all other columns** on the column **Categories**. To expand a column again, just click on it. To expand all of them and go back to the initial view, see the *Moving columns around* section in this recipe.

| ▼ All | | | | ▼ Categories | | | |
|---|---|---|---|---|---|---|---|
| ☆ ◁ | 1. | | | Botanical specimens\|Numismatics | | | |
| ☆ ◁ | 2. | | | Specimens\|Mineral Samples-Geological\|Mineral samples | | | |
| ☆ ◁ | 3. | | | Pearl shells\|Didactic displays\|Buttons\|Didactic Displays | | | |
| ☆ ◁ | 4. | | | Scientific Instruments | | | |
| ☆ ◁ | 5. | | | Domestic Equipment-Home\|Coal boxes | | | |
| ☆ ◁ | 6. | | | Botanical specimens\|Botanical Specimens\|Didactic Displays\|Models | | | |
| ☆ ◁ | 7. | | | Building Equipment and Materials\|Building stones | | | |
| ☆ ◁ | 8. | | | Botanical specimens\|Botanical Specimens\|Models | | | |
| ☆ ◁ | 9. | | | Building Equipment and Materials\|Building stones | | | |
| ☆ ◁ | 10. | | | Geological specimens\|Mineral Samples-Geological | | | |

# Moving columns around

In some cases, it might be useful to change the order of the columns from the original file, for instance, to bring together columns that need to be compared. To achieve this, enter the menu of the chosen column and click on **Edit column**. Again, four options are available at the bottom of the submenu:

- Move column to beginning
- Move column to end
- Move column to left
- Move column to right

If you want to reorder the columns completely, use the first column called **All**. This column allows you to perform operations on several columns at the same time. The **View** option offers a quick way to collapse or expand all columns, while **Edit columns | Re-order / remove columns...** is an efficient way to rearrange columns by dragging them around or suppressing them by dropping them on the right, as shown in the following screenshot:

| Drag columns to re-order | Drop columns here to remove |
|---|---|
| Record ID | Registration Number |
| Object Title | Provenance (Production) |
| Description | Provenance (History) |
| Marks | Persistent Link |
| Categories | Depth |
| Height | Diameter |
| Width | Production Date |
| Weight | |
| License info | |

# Renaming and removing columns

Under the same **Edit column** menu item, you also have the possibility to:

- Rename this column
- Remove this column

You could use renaming to suppress the unnecessary dot at the end of the **Description** column header, for instance. Removing a column is clearly more radical than simply collapsing it, but this can nevertheless be reversed, as you will learn by reading *Recipe 5 – using the project history*.

# Recipe 5 – using the project history

In this recipe, you will learn how you can go back in time at any point in the project's life and how to navigate through the history even if your project has been closed and opened again.

A very useful feature of OpenRefine is its handling of the history of all modifications that affected the data since the creation of the project. In practice, this means that you should never be afraid to try out things: do feel free at all times to fiddle with your data and to apply any transformation that crosses your mind, since everything can be undone in case you realize that it was a mistake (even if months have passed since the change was made).

To access the project history, click on the **Undo / Redo** tab in the top-left of the screen, just next to the **Facet / Filter** one, as shown in the following screenshot:

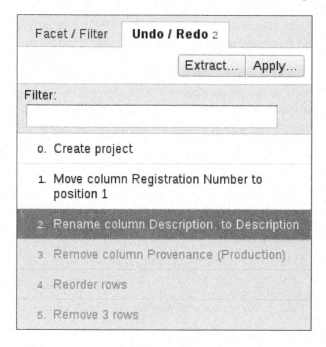

In order to turn back the clock, click on the last step that you want to be maintained. For instance, to cancel the removal of the column **Provenance (Production)** and all subsequent steps, click on **2. Rename column Description. to Description**. Step 2 will be highlighted, and steps 3 to 5 will be grayed out. This means that the renaming will be kept, but not the next three steps. To cancel all changes and recover the data as they were before any transformation was made, click on **0. Create project**. To undo the cancellation (redo), click on the step up to which you want to restore the history: for instance, click on **4. Reorder rows** to apply steps 3 and 4 again, while maintaining the suppression of step 5 (rows removing).

Be cautious, however, that going back and doing something else will erase all subsequent steps. For instance, if you go back from step 5 to step 2 and then choose to move the column **Description** on the left, step 3 will now read **3. Move column description to position 1** and the gray steps in the preceding screenshot will disappear for good: you cannot have two conflicting histories recorded at the same time. Be sure to experiment with this in order to avoid nasty surprises in the future.

It is important to notice that only the operations actually affecting data are listed in the project history. Visual aids such as switching between the rows and records view, displaying less or more records on a page, or collapsing and expanding columns again, are not really transformations and are therefore not saved. A consequence is that they will be lost from one session to the other: when you come back to a project that was previously closed, all columns will be expanded again, whereas renamed and removed columns will still be the way you left them last time, along with every other operation stored in the project history. In *Chapter 2, Analyzing and Fixing Data*, we will see that this is also true for other types of operations: while cell and column transformations are registered in the history, filters and facets are not.

Note that operation history can also be extracted in JSON format by clicking on the **Extract...** button just under **Undo / Redo**. This will allow you to select the steps you want to extract (note that only reusable operations can be extracted, which excludes operations performed on specific cells), which will then be converted into JSON automatically and can then be copy-pasted. Steps 1 and 2 from the preceding screenshot would be expressed as:

```
[
  {
    "op": "core/column-move",
    "description": "Move column Registration Number to position
      1",
    "columnName": "Registration Number",
    "index": 1
  },
  {
    "op": "core/column-rename",
    "description": "Rename column Description. to Description",
    "oldColumnName": "Description.",
    "newColumnName": "Description"
  }
]
```

**Downloading the example files**

You can download the example files for all Packt books you have purchased from your account at http://www.packtpub.com. If you purchased this book elsewhere, you can visit http://www.packtpub.com/support and register to have the files e-mailed directly to you.

In the preceding code, op stands for operation, description actually describes what the operation does, and other variables are parameters passed to the operation (function). Steps that were previously saved as JSON in a text file can subsequently be reapplied to the same or another project by clicking on the **Apply...** button and pasting the extracted JSON history in the text area. Finally, in case you have performed several hundreds of operations and are at a loss to find some specific step, you can use the **Filter** field to restrict the history to the steps matching a text string. A filter on remove, for instance (or even on rem), would limit the displayed history to steps 3 and 5.

# Recipe 6 – exporting a project

In this recipe, you will explore the various ways to save your modified data in order to reuse them in other contexts, including **templating** that allows for any custom export format to be used.

Although you may already have moved, renamed, or even removed columns, none of these modifications have been saved to your original dataset (that is, the chapter1.tsv file from *Recipe 1 – installing OpenRefine* has been left untouched). In fact, unlike most spreadsheet softwares that directly record changes into the files opened with them, OpenRefine always works in memory on an internal copy of the data. While this is an extra safety catch, it also means that any modified data needs to be exported before they are shared with others or injected in another application. The **Export** menu in the top-right of the screen allows you to do just that:

| Export project |
| --- |
| Tab-separated value |
| Comma-separated value |
| HTML table |
| Excel |
| ODF spreadsheet |
| Triple loader |
| MQL Write |
| Custom tabular exporter... |
| Templating... |
| RDF as RDF/XML |
| RDF as Turtle |

Most options propose to convert the data back into the file formats that were used during importation, such as CSV and TSV, Excel and Open Document, and different flavors of RDF. Let's have a closer look at other choices though:

- **Export project**: This option allows you to export a zipped OpenRefine project in its internal format that can be shared with other people and imported on other machines or simply used for backup purposes.

- **HTML table**: This option comes in handy if you want to publish your cleaned data online.

- **Triple loader and MQLWrite**: This option has advanced options that require you to align the data to pre-existent schemas through the Freebase extension (there is more about that in *Appendix, Regular Expressions and GREL*).

- **Custom tabular exporter and templating**: Maybe most interesting to you, OpenRefine lets you have a tight control on how your data are effectively exported by selecting and ordering columns, omitting blank rows and choosing the precise format of dates and reconciliation results (see *Appendix, Regular Expressions and GREL* again), and so on, as you can see in the next screenshot:

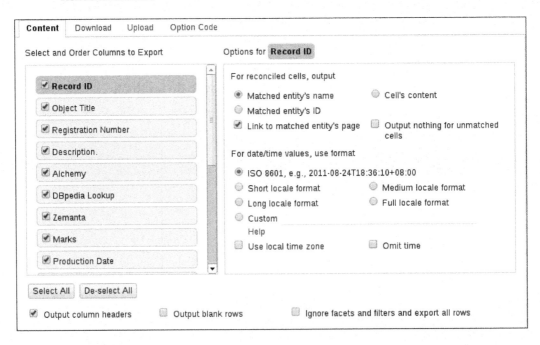

- **Templating...**: For even more control, you can use your own personal template by typing the desired format once, which will then be applied to all cells. In the following code, `cells["Record ID"].value`, for instance, corresponds to the actual value of each cell in the **Record ID** column which is then transformed into JSON, but could just as easily be formatted otherwise as shown in the following code snippet:

```
{
  "Record ID" : {{jsonize(cells["Record ID"].value)}},
  "Object Title" : {{jsonize(cells["Object
    Title"].value)}},
  "Registration Number" : {{jsonize(cells["Registration
    Number"].value)}},
  "Description. " : {{jsonize
    (cells["Description. "].value)}},
  "Marks" : {{jsonize(cells["Marks"].value)}},
  "Production Date" : {{jsonize(cells["Production
    Date"].value)}},
}
```

# Recipe 7 – going for more memory

In this last recipe, you will learn how to allocate more memory to the application in order to deal with larger datasets.

For large datasets, you might find that OpenRefine is performing slowly or shows you OutOfMemory errors. This is a sign that you should allocate more memory to the OpenRefine process. Unfortunately, this is a bit more complicated than the other things we have done so far, as it involves a bit of low-level fiddling. But don't worry: we'll guide you through it. The steps are different for each platform. A word of caution: the maximum amount of memory you can assign depends on the amount of RAM in your machine and whether you are using the 32 bit or 64 bit version of Java. When in doubt, try to increase the amount of memory gradually (for instance, in steps of 1024 MB) and check the result first.

## Windows

On Windows, you will have to edit the `openrefine.14j.ini` file in OpenRefine's main folder. Find the line that starts with -Xmx (which is Java speak for "maximum heap size"), which will show the default allocated memory: 1024M (meaning 1024 MB or 1 GB). Increase this as you see fit, for instance to 2048 M. The new settings will be in effect the next time you start OpenRefine.

# Mac

The instructions for Mac are a bit more complicated, as this operating system hides the configuration files from sight. After closing OpenRefine, hold control and click on its icon, selecting **Show package contents** from the pop-up menu. Then, open the `info.plist` file from the `Contents` folder. You should now see a list of OpenRefine settings. Navigate to the Java settings and edit the value of `VMOptions` (these are the properties of the Java Virtual Machine). Look for the part that starts with `-Xmx` and change its default value of 1024 M to the desired amount of memory, for instance, `-Xmx2048M`.

# Linux

This might come in as a surprise, but increasing allocated memory is easiest in Linux. Instead of starting OpenRefine with `./refine` as you usually would do, just type in `./refine -m 2048M`, where 2048 is the desired amount of memory in MB. To make the change permanent, you can create an alias in the hidden `.bashrc` file located in your home folder by adding the following line at the end of the file:

```
alias refine='cd path_to_refine ; ./refine -m 2048M'
```

Here, `path_to_refine` is the relative path from your home folder to the OpenRefine folder. Then, the next time you start OpenRefine with `./refine`, it will be allocated 2 GB by default.

# Summary

In this chapter, you have got to know OpenRefine, your new best friend for data profiling, cleaning, transformation, and many other things that you are still to discover. You now have an OpenRefine installation running and you know how to import your data into it by creating a new project and how to export them again after you are done. The mechanisms of rows and columns do not have any secrets for you any longer, and you understand how to navigate in the project history. You have also mastered memory allocation, which allows you to work on larger datasets.

Although it is always important to first have a good overview of what is in your dataset before dirtying your hands, you may now be getting impatient to perform actual changes on your data. If so, you are ready for *Chapter 2, Analyzing and Fixing Data*, which will move on to teach you the ins and outs of all the basic operations needed to analyze and fix your data.

# 2
# Analyzing and Fixing Data

In this chapter, we will go deeper into OpenRefine and review most of its basic functionalities intended for data fixing and analysis. We will cover the following topics, spread over six recipes:

- Recipe 1 – sorting data
- Recipe 2 – faceting data
- Recipe 3 – detecting duplicates
- Recipe 4 – applying a text filter
- Recipe 5 – using simple cell transformations
- Recipe 6 – removing matching rows

Even more so than in *Chapter 1, Diving Into OpenRefine*, the recipes are designed to allow readers to jump from one recipe to another in any way you like, depending on your needs and interests. Flowing reading of the chapter is also possible of course, but not mandatory at all.

Be warned that recipes are unequal in length; some are quite short and to the point, but others could not be constricted to one or two pages. *Recipe 2 – faceting data*, for instance, which covers the broad topic of faceting, runs over many pages and is divided into subrecipes.

 To follow the examples used throughout this chapter, we recommend that you load the chapter2.openrefine.tar.gz file directly by selecting **Import Project** at startup. Alternatively, you can work with your own OpenRefine project created from the chapter1.tsv file, as explained in *Chapter 1, Diving Into OpenRefine*.

# Recipe 1 – sorting data

In this recipe, you will learn how to sort data as a visual aid and how to reorder rows permanently as a prerequisite for more advanced operations.

Because sorted values are easier to explore and manipulate, sorting data is certainly something you will want to do at some point when working with OpenRefine; you can either use the sorted values as a visual aid or reorder your records permanently. In order to sort your data by their **Record ID**, for instance, choose **Sort...** in the column menu to access the following window:

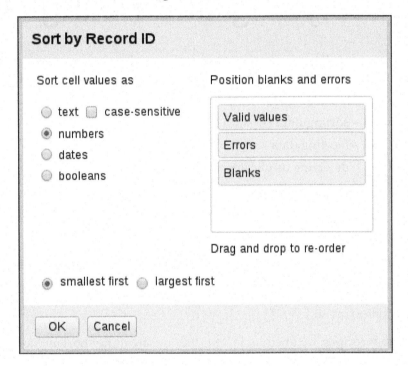

Cell values can be sorted according to their type: text (case-sensitive or not), numbers, dates, or Boolean values. For each type, we are offered two possible sorting orders:

- **Text**: alphabetical (a to z) or reversed alphabetical (z to a)
- **Numbers**: smallest first or largest first
- **Dates**: earliest first or latest first
- **Booleans**: false then true or true then false

Moreover, we can select where errors and blanks will be stored in relation to the valid values by dragging them in the desired order. For instance, errors could be sorted first (to spot them more easily) and blank values at the end (since they interest us less) with valid (normal) values in the middle.

Sorting the data by **Records ID** by selecting **numbers** and **smallest** first, for instance, will give the new ordering **7**, **9**, **14**, and so on, where you formerly had **267220**, **346260**, **267098**, and so on. The following screenshot illustrates the order before and after sorting:

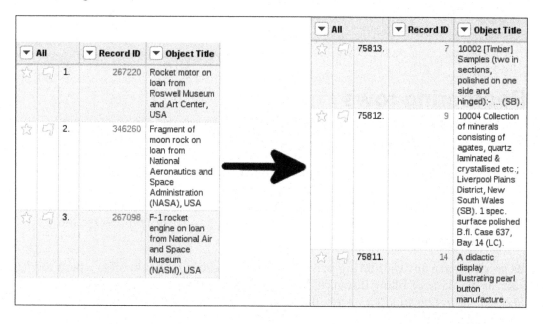

Sorting as **text** would have produced a different ordering starting with 100, 1001, 10019, and so on. Notice, however, that this sorting has not been recorded in the project history; you can check that yourself by clicking on the **Undo / Redo** tab in the top-left of the screen.

This is because the default behavior of sorting in OpenRefine is not to affect the data, but only to display them in any way you like, such as the rows/records alternation or the collapsing of unwanted columns (you may also think of sort filters in spreadsheet software). So every time you sort your data on a given column, you are faced with three options: to remove your sorting and go back to the original order, to keep it as a temporary visual aid, or to make the reordering permanent.

These options cannot be selected in the original column menu, but are available in a dedicated **Sort** menu appearing at the top as shown in the following screenshot:

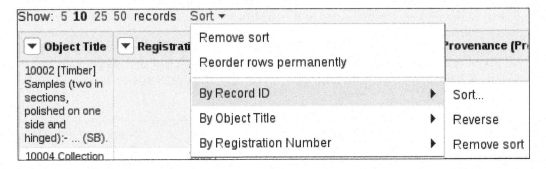

# Reordering rows

The **Sort** menu allows you to remove the sorting or to reorder rows permanently. In addition, it reminds you of what columns were used for the sorting, which makes it possible to combine various **sort** criteria (see the preceding screenshot). For instance, you could sort your data first on **Registration Number** then on **Object Title** as a double visual aid. Later, you could decide to remove the sort on the numbers only (by navigating to **Sort** | **By Registration Number** | **Remove sort**) and make the sort on the titles permanent. The individual sort submenus also let you reverse the sort order with one click.

Be sure to make any reordering permanent if you need it for some other operation, such as blanking or filling down cells, in order to avoid inconsistent results. In *Recipe 3 – detecting duplicates*, we will see how to use sorting as a preliminary step to removing duplicates.

# Recipe 2 – faceting data

One of the functionalities of OpenRefine that you will use most often is faceting. Facets do not affect the values of your data, but they allow you to get useful insights of your dataset; you can think of facets as various ways to look at your data, just like the facets of a gemstone that still have to be refined. Facets also allow you to apply a transformation to a subset of your data, as they allow you to display only rows corresponding to a given criterion.

In this recipe, we will explore the various ways of faceting data depending on their values and on your needs: text facets for strings, numeric facets for numbers and dates, a few predefined customized facets, and finally how to use stars and flags. Most of the power of OpenRefine lies in the ability to combine these different types of facets.

# Text facets

If your dataset has a column containing cities or country names, for instance, you will want to see at a glance what the different values are for that field and the number of occurrences for each one. This is exactly what text facets are for. Of course, faceting is only useful when a limited number of choices are at hand; it does not make sense to list all the object titles or descriptions, as it is very unlikely that they will appear twice (except in the case of duplicates, which will be dealt with in the next recipe).

The best candidate for text faceting in the **Powerhouse** collection is obviously the **Categories** column, as it contains keywords from a controlled vocabulary (called the **Powerhouse museum Object Name Thesaurus**, if you are curious). To put it simply, categories are a set of a few thousand terms used to describe the objects in the collection.

So, let's try to get an overview of these categories by navigating to **Facet | Text facet** in the **Categories** column menu. The result of this facet appears in the **Facet/Filter** tab on the left of the screen. Too bad; OpenRefine informs us that there are a total of 14,805 choices, which is far too much to display for memory's sake. In fact, the default upper bound for facet choices is only 2,000. We could attempt to get over this limitation by clicking on the **Set choice count limit** link and raising the upper limit to 15,000, for instance, but beware that this is likely to slow down the application, especially if you did not change the default RAM allocation (refer to *Recipe 7 – going for more memory*, of *Chapter 1, Diving Into OpenRefine*).

If you choose to raise the limit in the pop-up window, what OpenRefine really does is change the value of a Java variable called ui.browsing.listFacet.limit. While in most cases you will not need to bother about this barbaric name, it might come in handy if you realize that you increased the value too much and want to get it down again. In fact, OpenRefine will always offer to step up when the choice count oversteps the mark, but never the opposite. To do that, go to the system preferences at http://127.0.0.1:3333/preferences, edit the preference with key ui.browsing.listFacet.limit, and set its value to something smaller. To go back to the default 2000 value, you can also delete this preference altogether.

Instead, click on the **Facet by choice counts** link just below, which will open a second facet under the first one. This new facet, which is also on the **Categories** column, will allow you to restrict the range of categories to be displayed in the first text facet. When it first opens, OpenRefine tries to show all categories, whether they appear only once in the collection or several thousand times. Since there are too many categories to display, it makes sense to focus on the most popular ones, in the first phase at least.

Drag the left handle to increase the lower limit to 1000 instead of 0. The preceding text facet refreshes automatically, and now the categories shown are only those that are used to describe at least 1000 objects in the collection. There are only 7 of them, which is a lot easier to display and to browse. To get an even better picture, you can choose to sort them by **count** (from most frequent to least frequent) instead of by **name** (alphabetically).

The following screenshot shows what you should now have in your two facets:

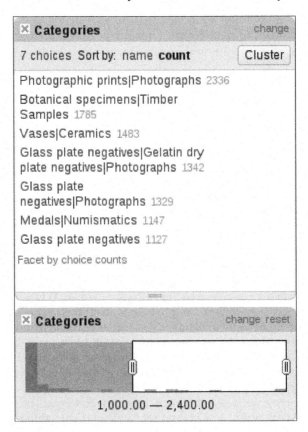

If you want to export these seven top categories, just click on the **7 choices** link and you will get them as nice **tab separated values** (TSV), ready to copy and paste in your favorite text editor or spreadsheet. However, most of these categories are looking very suspicious. As a matter of fact, **Photographic prints | Photographs** is not a single category, but rather two categories separated by a vertical bar, or pipe character ( | ).

This is exactly why we had so many choices in the first place. As a result, **Glass plate negatives | Gelatin dry plate negatives | Photographs**, **Glass plate negatives | Photographs**, and **Glass plate negatives** are all listed as distinct choices even though they contain the same category. This, however, is the plague of multivalued cells, and we are not ready for dealing with them right now. We will have to wait until *Chapter 3*, *Advanced Data Operations*, where we will also learn more about this intriguing **Cluster** button that we have ignored purposefully for the time being.

As the faceting of categories was somewhat skewed, let's have a quick look at another text facet before moving on to numeric ones. The choice of column is less obvious, but we can see that the **Height** field does not contain only numbers, but also numbers followed by units of measurement, such as **990 mm**. This means that we will not be able to apply a numeric facet to this column (or at least, not straightforwardly), but we can try with a text facet, hoping that there will not be too many different values to display.

Fortunately, navigating to **Facet | Text facet** from the **Height** column menu informs us that there are 1313 choices, well under the 2000 default limit. Sorting them by **count** instead of **name** reveals the surprising fact that **1368** objects in the collection have a height of exactly **164 mm**, whereas the second most frequent size of **215 mm** is only found in **400** objects. These values can be found in the following screenshot:

At the bottom of that list, we can also see that 45501 objects have a blank value for **Height**, which means that no height has been recorded for them. However, we will not linger with them now, since OpenRefine offers us a special facet for dealing with blank rows which we will discover when we talk about customized facets.

# Numeric facets

Finding a column that is relevant for a numeric facet is quite easier than for text facets, as several of them contain numerals. Numbers are easily spotted as they are colored in green, assuming the **Parse cell text into numbers, dates...**, checkbox was selected at the time of the project creation. The **Record ID** column is as good a choice as any, as a facet will allow us to have an overview of the distribution of IDs, and to check that all objects have one.

In the **Record ID** column menu, navigate to **Facet | Numeric facet** and look at what appears in the **Facet/Filter** tab on the left. Whereas a text facet returned a list of different choices, numeric facets yield ranges of values, just like the one we had when faceting by choice counts.

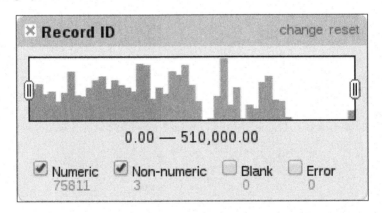

We can see that the values for the **Record ID** column range from **0** to **510,000**, with a small gap between 270,000 and 280,000, and a larger one between 410,000 and 500,000. By sliding the handles, we can have a closer look at the 533 rows that have an ID superior to 500,000, for instance.

Under the graph, the values are divided into four categories: **Numeric, Non-numeric, Blank**, and **Errors** resulting from a problematic operation. No errors were found since we did not modify these values yet, and no blanks were found either, which means that all objects in the collections have been assigned a record ID. However, three rows have a non-numeric value, which is unexpected for an ID. Let's find out more about these rows by deselecting the **Numeric** checkbox, leaving only the **Non-numeric** one checked.

On the right, we can now ██████████bing rows. Not only do they lack a
record ID, but all other ████████████t for a persistent link to the
object and the license i████████████████natically. These rows do
not represent actual o████████████████afely removed
(we will see how in t████████████

However, somethin███████████████████y were they
categorized as non████████████████████**Blank** checkbox?
Whitespace is the████████████████████e three cells. To
do that, just how████████████████████**cord ID** column
and a small **edi**████████████████████ for yourself that
they contain a████████████████████ot:

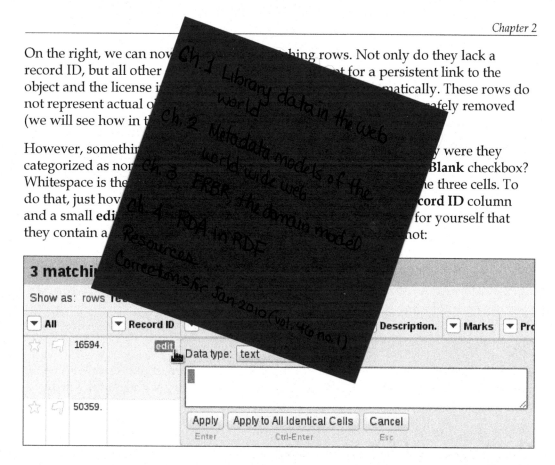

To correct this, remove the problematic whitespace by hitting the *Backspace* or *Delete*
key then click on the **Apply to All Identical Cells** button below or press *Ctrl + Enter*.
OpenRefine informs you on top of the screen in a yellow box that three cells have
been mass-edited in the column **Record ID**. As a result, the facet on the left refreshes
and the three cells in question switched to the Blank box.

Before moving to customized facets, let's quickly mention two other ways for
faceting that are related to the numeric facet: the timeline facet and scatterplot facet.

A timeline facet requires dates, so text strings such as 17/10/1890 need to be
converted to the date format first. You can try that on the **Production Date** column,
but notice that real dates are a minority, since it also contains years such as 1984 and
ranges such as 2006 to 2007. We can nonetheless navigate to **Edit cells | Common
transforms | To date** in that column menu, transforming 79 cells into date format;
for instance, 17/10/1890 will be converted to 1890-10-17T00:00:00Z, with the zeros
indicating the time of day in hours, minutes, and seconds.

Clearly, 79 cells out of a total of 75,814 is not a lot, but a timeline facet on these values would still show objects created on a given date range from 26 February, 1880 to 31 January, 1952, while most values are either not time expressions (19,820) or blank (55,915).

The following screenshot shows what can be obtained with a timeline facet on the **Production Date** column after converting dates to OpenRefine's internal time format:

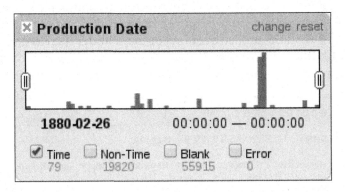

Finally, scatterplot facets allow for a graphical representation of numerical values. We won't go into the details of this particular facet, but do try it yourself if you are curious about it.

## Customized facets

We have now seen the two main types of facets, text facets and numeric facets, but many and more of them exist, and you could think of almost any way of faceting the data depending on your needs. Custom facets allow you to do just that; defining your own facets, whether text ones (for instance, faceting on the first character of a string), or numeric ones (for instance, faceting on the square root of a number). However, they require a basic understanding of the **General Refine Expression Language** (**GREL**), which will be introduced in *Appendix, Regular Expressions and GREL*.

Yet, OpenRefine also provides a few customized facets; these are predefined custom facets that have proved to be of a common use to many users. In what follows, we will browse these facets, paying particular attention to the most useful of them. Let's first have a quick look at the **Customized facets** submenu, which can be accessed from any column:

| |
|---|
| Word facet |
| Duplicates facet |
| Numeric log facet |
| 1-bounded numeric log facet |
| Text length facet |
| Log of text length facet |
| Unicode char-code facet |
| Facet by error |
| Facet by blank |

**Word facet** lists all the different words used in a field, a word being simplistically defined as a text string between two whitespace characters. This is something you will want to try on a subset of your data, as the number of choices can quickly grow very large; a word facet on the column **Description**, for instance, would display 212,751 different words, which is a sure way to crash the application.

Word facets could be used to refine your list of categories. For instance, while a simple text facet will tell you how many objects were described as cocktail dresses, a word facet will split that category into two words, and let you browse separately the various dresses on one hand and the objects related to cocktail (including cocktail glasses for instance) on the other hand.

**Duplicates facet** allows you to detect duplicate values; so we will keep that for the next recipe.

**Numeric log facet** is a shortcut to display the logarithm of numbers instead of their actual values, which can be useful if your data follows a power law distribution. The **1-bounded numeric log facet** is the same, except that it does not accept values under one.

**Text length facet** organizes the objects according to the number of characters contained in some string, the **Object Title** for instance. Navigating to **Facet | Customized facets | Text length facet** in that column menu will show you that the titles range from 0 to 260 characters. You can then focus on the 92 titles that are shorter than 10 characters (no more than a word in most cases, and not very informative) or on the 2007 titles that are longer than 250 characters (which are often redundant with descriptions).

Speaking of descriptions, an analysis of their length is also of interest, but the distribution is so large (ranging from 0 to 4,100 characters, although 85 percent of the descriptions are shorter than 500 characters) that it is quite difficult to make sense of it. This is where the log of text length facet (the following screenshot) comes into the picture, allowing for a much clearer chart:

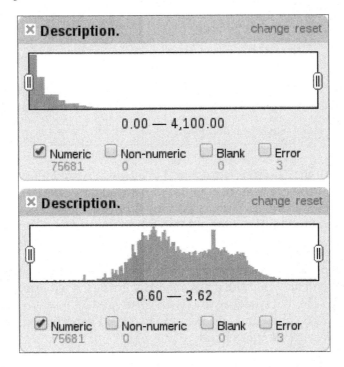

The **Unicode char-code facet** does not compute a string's length, but lists all the characters used in the string. Try that on the **Object Title** column for instance; most English characters are under 128, but accented letters from other European languages can range up to 256, or even higher for Arabic or Chinese characters, for instance. If you notice suspiciously high values, however, it could mean that OpenRefine did not recognize your dataset's encoding properly. In this case, start again with a new project and select the right encoding manually.

Finally, you can facet your data by error (assuming they contain any), or facet them by blank. This last option is very useful to know what proportion of the collection has been filled for a given field, and can often be used in combination with another facet. A quick glance at the **Marks** column shows that the first few cells are empty, so we could navigate to **Facet | Customized facets | Facet by blank** to learn more about it. This facet informs us that 18,968 values are false (that is, not blank), and 56,846 are true (that is, blank). In other words, only a quarter of the objects have some marks described in the file.

Even more significant is that the column **Weight** (on the right, use the horizontal scrollbar to view it) has only been filled for 179 objects, leaving it empty in 99.998 percent of cases. And faceting by blank on the object titles shows that 118 records are dummies; they got a record ID along with a persistent link and some fake license information based on this ID, but all the other columns are empty, so they do not really refer to an object.

# Faceting by star or flag

In *Chapter 1, Diving Into OpenRefine*, we briefly mentioned the existence of stars and flags in the special **All** column on the left. It is now time to see how these can be used as well to facet your data in meaningful ways. Stars can be used to mark good rows or favorite rows that you want to pick up in order to come back to them later; conversely, flags can be used to indicate bad rows or problematic rows that will need special attention further on. Note that this is just a suggestion; you could use stars and flags to mean something completely different.

To star or flag a single row, just click on the corresponding symbol on the left. Most of the time, however, you will want to mark multiple rows in one go. To do that, you first need to isolate these rows in the display, often by using another facet. For instance, you could detect empty rows by going to the **Registration Number** column menu and navigating to **Facet | Customized facets | Facet by blank**, and clicking on **true** on the left in order to display the 118 matching (empty) rows only. To flag them all, open the **All** column menu and navigate to **Edit rows | Flag rows**. The same works for stars, and you can unflag and unstar multiple rows as well in the same menu.

Now imagine that you want to display the rows that have some information about the diameter *or* their weight. If you facet by blank on both columns at the same time and click on **false** twice, you will end with only 29 matching rows which correspond to those having a diameter *and* a weight recorder in the dataset. To achieve what we want, the solution is to proceed in two steps: facet by blank on the column **Diameter**, and select the 2106 rows marked as false (that is, for which the diameter is present) and star them with **All | Edit rows | Star rows**. Clear the facet and repeat these steps with the 179 rows from the **Weight** column (you may notice that only 150 rows are effectively starred, the 29 remaining ones having already been starred since they have both measurements). Clear the facet again and display what we were looking for by navigating to **All | Facet | Facet by star**. The same works for flags, of course.

Hooray, we have reached the end of this long recipe at last! It may have felt somewhat disproportionate, but facets are really the ABC of OpenRefine, so it was worth the effort.

# Recipe 3 – detecting duplicates

In this recipe, you will learn what duplicates are, how to spot them, and why it matters.

The only type of customized facet that we left out in the previous recipe is the duplicates facet. Duplicates are annoying records that happen to appear twice (or more) in a dataset. Keeping identical records is a waste of space and can generate ambiguity, so we will want to remove these duplicates. This facet is an easy way to detect them, but it has a downside; it only works on text strings, at least straightforwardly (to learn how to tweak it to work on integers as well, have a look at *Appendix, Regular Expressions and GREL*).

Too bad then; we cannot use a duplicate facet on the Record ID column. The next best thing is to run it on the registration numbers, which are an internal classification of objects in the collection, though they are not as reliable as the IDs, since they have an extrinsic meaning for collection managers. Anyway, let's give it a try by navigating to **Registration Number | Facet | Customized facets | Duplicates facet**; 281 rows are marked as duplicates, and we can display them by clicking on the word **true** in the facet on the left.

Now scroll down some rows to have a look at those duplicates. We see there is a problem; the duplicates facet included all the blank rows which are indeed the same, but not duplicates of an object since they do not represent any. To exclude these 118 empty rows, we need another facet that can be accessed through **Registration Number | Facet | Customized facets | Facet by blank**. Click on **false** to keep the 163 real duplicates and notice that the first facet above refreshes automatically.

Finally, add a third facet, a simple text facet this time, to list the different registration numbers that feature more than once in the dataset. Sorting by count, we can see that out of the 79 choices, 77 are indeed strict duplicates (values present twice), whereas one value appears thrice (**2008/37/1**), and one as many as six times (**86/1147-3**). The three facets can be seen in the following screenshot:

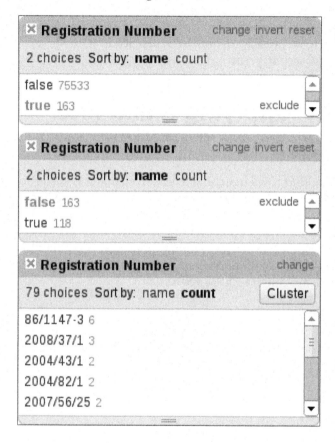

Now back to our record IDs. Since the duplicates facet is of no use on integers, we will use a workaround to detect duplicates in that column. To achieve that, we will first sort the data on their IDs by navigating to **Record ID | Sort...** and toggling **numbers** and **smallest first**. As you may recall from *Chapter 1, Diving Into OpenRefine*, sorting is but a visual aid, so the reordering needs to be made permanent by going to the **Sort** menu that has just appeared (right of **Show: 5 10 25 50 rows**), and clicking on **Reorder rows permanently**. If you forget to reorder the rows, further operations will ignore the sorting and yield unexpected results.

Now that the rows are sorted by ID, duplicates will necessarily be grouped together, so we can navigate to **Record ID** | **Edit cells** | **Blank down** to replace the IDs of duplicate rows by blanks (every original row will keep its ID, only subsequent ones will lose them). Faceting the blanked rows by navigating to **Record ID** | **Facet** | **Customized facets** | **Facet by blank** will display the 86 redundant rows (or maybe 84 if you already removed blank rows) including one row from each pair, two of the triplet, and five of the sextuplet. These 86 rows are the real duplicates without the original rows to be preserved, and we will learn how to remove them in *Recipe 6 – removing matching rows*.

# Recipe 4 – applying a text filter

In this recipe, you will learn about filters that allow you to search for values displaying some patterns.

When you want to find rows matching a certain string, it is easier to rely on a simple text filter than on cumbersome facets. Let's start with a simple example. Suppose you want to filter all titles relating to the United States. Navigate to **Object Title** | **Text filter** and watch the filter box open on the left, in the same tab where facets appear. Now type in USA. OpenRefine tells you that there are 1,866 matching rows. Select the **case sensitive** checkbox to eliminate happenstance matches, such as karakusa and Jerusalem, and we are down to 1,737 rows:

Still, we cannot be sure that there is no noise left in these matches; there could be occurrences of JERUSALEM in capital letters for instance. To get around this problem, we could try to add spaces to either side of USA, but at the risk of losing cases, such as [USA] or /USA, along with occurrences of the beginning or the end of a title. As a matter of fact, the filter  USA  with whitespace only returns 172 matches, about one-tenth of all occurrences of USA, which is a lot of silence.

On the other side of the coin, our simple text filter does not account for spellings such as U.S.A. (201 matches), U S A (29 matches), or U.S.A (22 matches). It can quickly become a nightmare to keep track of all the variants, and you will need to star the rows individually in order to group them all together later.

This is where regular expressions come into the picture. Regexes, as they are often called, are extremely powerful, but they demand a basic understanding of their peculiar syntax before they can be used fruitfully. For instance, an expression such as \bU.?S.?A\b (with the regular expression box selected) would match all preceding relevant cases while excluding problematic ones, and would return 1,978 matching rows.

It is beyond the scope of this recipe to teach you how to master regexes, but *Appendix, Regular Expressions and GREL,* is waiting for you to explain the basics.

Another useful thing we can do with text filters is checking the aptness of separators. In the **Categories** column, pipe characters ( | ) are used to single out categories. Let's add a text filter on that column and start by typing a single pipe. OpenRefine displays 71105 matching rows, which means that most of the objects are described with at least two categories (since a single category does not need a pipe separator).

Now add a second pipe to get | |; nine problematic rows are detected containing a double pipe instead of a single one. In *Chapter 3, Advanced Data Operations,* we will see how to use the GREL to fix this issue. Another problem is cells beginning or ending with a pipe, but finding them requires the use of regular expressions as well, so that will have to wait until *Appendix, Regular Expressions and GREL.*

# Recipe 5 – using simple cell transformations

In this recipe, you will learn how to use OpenRefine's built-in transformations to modify subsets of your data.

When playing with facets and filters, we have essentially displayed the data in various ways, but we have not really affected them. Now comes the time to modify your data at last, and this means entering the powerful **Edit cells** menu. While we already used **Blank down** in order to detect duplicates, other transformations, such as splitting and joining multi-valued cells or clustering and editing values, are more advanced, so we will delay their discussion until the next chapter. Other transforms are easier to grasp; however, we will focus now on those available through the **Common transforms** submenu pictured in the following screenshot:

| Trim leading and trailing whitespace |
| Collapse consecutive whitespace |
| Unescape HTML entities |
| To titlecase |
| To uppercase |
| To lowercase |
| To number |
| To date |
| To text |
| Blank out cells |

**Trimming whitespace** at the beginning and end of a string is a good first step to improve the quality of your data. It will ensure that their identical values will not differ by leading and trailing whitespace only, which can be quite tricky to detect, making your data more consistent. It can also help reduce the size of your dataset by eliminating unnecessary characters; while a small space does not weigh much, several thousands of them can make a difference and cause hidden havoc. Remember the blank values that were categorized as non-numeric because of a single whitespace character.

Unique identifiers should not contain spaces either; let's check if all is well by navigating to **Registration Number | Edit cells | Common transforms | Trim leading and trailing whitespace**. 2,349 cells are affected by the operation, which means it was well needed. Note that we cannot do the same on the Record ID column, since trimming only works on strings, not on integers; the result would be to suppress all IDs!

**Consecutive whitespace** is also common when typing too fast, and we would expect to find some in long text fields such as object titles or descriptions. Surprisingly, these are not to be found in these columns, whereas running **Collapse consecutive whitespace** on the column **Production Date** reveals 7671 values affected, but these are mostly integers being converted to strings. Do try these two transformations on other columns for yourself; they are safe and can only prove beneficial for your data.

If your data were exported from some web application, it is likely that they will contain **HyperText Markup Language** (**HTML**) code. In HTML, special characters are escaped (that is, protected) by a number or with custom shortcuts known as HTML entities. For instance, the French é character (e with an acute accent) would be encoded either as `&#233;` or as `&eacute;` depending on the paradigm used.

While these are useful on the Web to avoid encoding problems in your browser, they can make reading difficult when they are not properly unescaped (unescaping `&eacute;` for instance would mean transforming it back into é). So, if you spot some of those values beginning with an ampersand (`&`) and ending with a semi-colon (`;`), go to **Edit cells | Common transforms | Unescape HTML entities** and watch your data being transformed into something legible.

The next family of transforms is **case transformations**; we can convert text strings to lowercase, UPPERCASE, or Titlecase. For instance, we could check that no lowercase letters are present in the registration numbers by navigating to **Registration Number | Edit cells | Common transforms | To uppercase**. 2,349 cells are transformed, which could mean huge quality issues, but it is in fact much ado about nothing. The values transformed were simply integers that were converted to strings in the process (since numbers do not have a case). You can check that for yourself by adding a numeric facet on the **Registration Number** column first, then launch the case transform and watch the numeric values vanish, replaced by a message informing you that no numeric values are present.

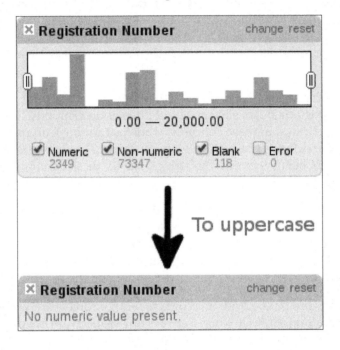

Similarly, we can use **To lowercase** to verify that no capital letters are present in the persistent link URL or **To titlecase** to standardize the spelling of categories, smoothing the difference between Didactic Displays and Didactic displays for instance. However, **To titlecase** only keeps capital letters after whitespace, so **Spacecraft|Models|Space Technology** would be transformed into **Spacecraft|models|space Technology**, which is far from ideal. Do not bother too much about that now, though, as *Chapter 3, Advanced Data Operations*, will introduce a better and more powerful way of dealing with such cases: clustering.

In *Recipe 2 – faceting data*, we used one of the type transformations available. In fact, you may remember that temporal expressions had to be converted to dates (that is, OpenRefine's internal format for dates, which is `yyyy-mm-ddThh:mm:ssZ`) before we could use a timeline facet on them. The same works for converting values to text or to numbers. We could transform record IDs into text, for instance, in order to be able to use a duplicates facet on them, but then we will need to convert them to numbers again before sorting them (to avoid 10 being put before 2) or working with numeric facets.

The last transformation predefined for us by OpenRefine is pretty blunt; **Blank out cells** does just that; it deletes all values in a given column. Of course, this is best used on a subset of the rows, not on the whole dataset. A useful combination would be to flag rows with problematic values for a given field, navigate to **All** | **Facet** | **Facet by flag**, and then blank out the cells from the matching rows.

We are now done with the common transforms, but be assured that this is only the tip of the iceberg; the possibilities of transformations are countless, as you will discover in *Chapter 3*, *Advanced Data Operations* and *Appendix*, *Regular Expressions and GREL*. In fact, **Edit cells** | **Transform...** opens the **Custom text transform** window, which lets you define your own transformation with GREL. This may sound frightening at first, but trust us that it is worth the trouble.

# Recipe 6 – removing matching rows

In this recipe, you will learn how to suppress problematic rows that have been previously singled out through the use of facets and filters.

Detecting duplicates or flagging redundant rows is fine, but it is only part of the job. At some point, you will want to cross the mark between **data profiling** (or analysis) and **data cleaning**. In practice, this means that rows that have been identified as inappropriate during the diagnosis phase (and probably flagged as such) will need to be removed from the dataset, since they are detrimental to its quality.

To remove rows, be sure to have a facet or filter in place first, otherwise you will remove all rows in the dataset. Let's start from the clean project again (import it for a second time or toggle the **Undo / Redo** tab and select **0. Create project** to cancel all modifications) and see what we can do to clean up this dataset. Also, check that OpenRefine shows your data as rows, not records.

We will first remove the rows lacking a record ID. To do that, navigate to **Record ID | Facet | Numeric facet** and deselect the **Numeric** checkbox from the facet opening in the left pane. This leaves us with only **Non-numeric** checked and three matching rows. Remember that **Facet by blank** would not have worked, since these three rows are not really blank, but have a single whitespace character in the **Record ID** cells. Now go to **All | Edit rows | Remove all matching rows** and watch the rows disappear.

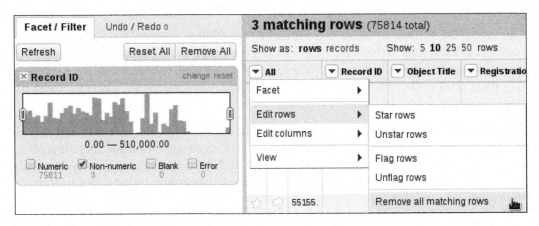

Well done, the dataset is three rows shorter, no non-numeric record IDs are left (as you can see in the facet that has been refreshed), and data quality has already been improved. Clear the facet and check that the total is down to 75,811 rows.

Next, we will handle rows without a registration number that are also suspicious in a museum collection. No spaces are in the way here (you can check that with a simple text filter on the column **Registration Number** by typing in a single whitespace character; no matching rows are found), so we can navigate to **Registration Number | Facet | Customized facets | Facet by blank**. Click on **true** on the left to select the 115 corresponding rows; they are all empty as well, so we can select **Remove all matching rows** again.

As you can see, removing blank rows is quite easy; we will now focus on duplicate rows. Duplicates are a bit trickier, as you may recall from *Recipe 3 – detecting duplicates*, but we want to get rid of them nonetheless. Start by navigating to **Registration Number | Facet | Customized facets | Duplicates facet** and click on **true** to see the 163 matching rows. The problem is, if we suppress all these rows, we will not only delete duplicates, but also original values. In other words, if a row appears twice in the dataset, removing all matching rows will delete both of them instead of just one. If this happens, remember you can always go back in the project history.

So, we need a way to remove duplicates while safeguarding original rows. This can be achieved in the following manner: sort on column **Registration Number**, selecting **text** and **a-z** as options (the **case sensitive** box need not be checked since there are only uppercase letters in this field), then reorder the rows based on that sorting by navigating to **Sort | Reorder rows permanently**. Finally, replace repeated values with a blank by navigating to **Registration Number | Edit cells | Blank down**, which should affect 84 cells.

If you left the duplicates facet open, you will witness it refreshed to display these 84 matching rows. What happened is that the original values (that were part of the 163) are now singled out, so they are no longer considered duplicates and swung to **false**. The real duplicates, however, have been blanked down, so they all have one and the same value now: blank. It is as if it were a big duplicate cluster of 84 rows. In any case, you can now remove these matching rows, leaving the original ones untouched.

If all went well, you should now be left with 75,612 rows. We could go on with other removals, but you probably have got the general idea by now, so we will leave it to you to experiment with other columns. Have a look at the project history in the **Undo / Redo** tab to review to steps that we have been through.

| Facet / Filter | **Undo / Redo** 5 | |
| --- | --- | --- |
| | Extract... | Apply... |

Filter:

0. Create project

1. Remove 3 rows

2. Remove 115 rows

3. Reorder rows

4. Blank down 84 cells in column Registration Number

5. Remove 84 rows

We first removed three blank rows followed by 115 further rows that were nearly blank but for their record ID. In order to remove the 84 duplicates, we had to reorder the rows and to blank them down on the column **Registration Number**. In total, we have deleted 202 rows, leaving our dataset that much cleaner. Notice that the text facets and sorting operations are not listed in the history, since they did not affect the data but only served as visual aids for performing the removals.

# Summary

During the course of this chapter, we have learned how to master the basics of OpenRefine in order to analyze and fix datasets, essential components of data profiling and cleaning.

Analyzing data involved sorting and the use of various facets, but also the application of text filters and the detection of duplicates.

Fixing data was accomplished through reordering, cell transformations, and deletion.

In the next chapter, we will bring our understanding of the inner workings of OpenRefine to another level by venturing into advanced data operations.

Suppose we want to give the **Categories** field a closer look to check how many different categories are there and which categories are the most prominent. First, let's see what happens if we try to create a text facet on this field by clicking on the dropdown next to **Categories** and navigating to **Facet | Text Facet** as shown in the following screenshot. As you might remember from *Chapter 2, Analyzing and Fixing Data* this doesn't work as expected because there are too many combinations of individual categories. OpenRefine simply gives up, saying that there are 14,805 choices in total, which is above the limit for display. While you can increase the maximum value by clicking on **Set choice count limit**, we strongly advise against this. First of all, it would make OpenRefine painfully slow as it would offer us a list of 14,805 possibilities, which is too large for an overview anyway. Second, it wouldn't help us at all because OpenRefine would only list the combined field values (such as Hen eggs|Sectional models|Animal Samples and Products). This does not allow us to inspect the individual categories, which is what we're interested in.

To solve this, leave the facet open, but go to the **Categories** dropdown again and select **Edit Cells | Split multi-valued cells...** as shown in the following screenshot:

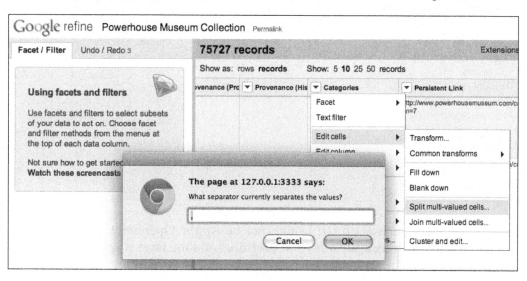

OpenRefine now asks **What separator currently separates the values?**. As we can see in the first few records, the values are separated by a vertical bar or pipe character, as the horizontal line tokens are called. Therefore, enter a vertical bar | in the dialog. If you are not able to find the corresponding key on your keyboard, try selecting the character from one of the Categories cells and copying it so you can paste it in the dialog. Then, click on **OK**.

After a few seconds, you will see that OpenRefine has split the cell values, and the **Categories** facet on the left now displays the individual categories. By default, it shows them in alphabetical order, but we will get more valuable insights if we sort them by the number of occurrences. This is done by changing the **Sort by** option from **name** to **count**, revealing the most popular categories.

One thing we can do now, which we couldn't do when the field was still multi-valued is changing the name of a single category across all records. For instance, to change the name of **Clothing and Dress**, hover over its name in the created **Categories** facet and click on the **edit** link, as you can see in the following screenshot:

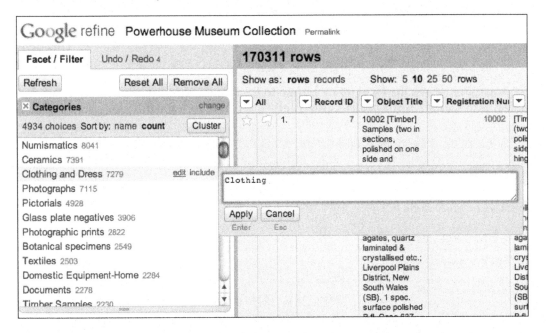

Enter a new name such as `Clothing` and click on **Apply**. OpenRefine changes all occurrences of **Clothing and Dress** into **Clothing**, and the facet is updated to reflect this modification.

Once you are done editing the separate values, it is time to merge them back together. Go to the **Categories** dropdown, navigate to **Edit cells | Join multi-valued cells...**, and enter the separator of your choice. This does not need to be the same separator as before, and multiple characters are also allowed. For instance, you could opt to separate the fields with a comma followed by a space.

# Recipe 2 – alternating between rows and records mode

Now let's have a look at how OpenRefine gives you access to multi-valued cells. When we follow the instructions of the previous recipe to split a column's values, we see that OpenRefine does two things. On one hand, it takes the first of the different values of a cell and puts it in the original row. On the other hand, it takes each of the remaining values and puts all of them in a cell of their own on an otherwise empty row. For instance, in the following screenshot, you can see that the record with ID **9** has been stretched out over three rows, each of which contains a category name. Only the first category is on a row that contains the other values of the field; the others are empty except for the category value (some columns have been hidden for clarity).

| 170311 rows | | | | |
|---|---|---|---|---|
| Show as: **rows** records    Show: 5 10 25 **50** rows | | | | |
| ☐ All | ▼ Record ID | ▼ Object Title | ▼ Categories | ▼ Persistent Link |
| ☆ ⤳ 1. | 7 | 0002 [Timber] Samples (two in... | Botanical specimens | http://www.powerhousemuseum.com/collection/database/?irn=7 |
| ☆ ⤳ 2. | | | Numismatics | |
| ☆ ⤳ 3. | 9 | 0004 Collection of minerals c... | Mineral samples | http://www.powerhousemuseum.com/collection/database/?irn=9 |
| ☆ ⤳ 4. | | | Specimens | |
| ☆ ⤳ 5. | | | Mineral Samples-Geological | |
| ☆ ⤳ 6. | 14 | didactic display illustratin... | Didactic displays | http://www.powerhousemuseum.com/collection/database/?irn=14 |
| ☆ ⤳ 7. | | | Pearl shells | |
| ☆ ⤳ 8. | | | Buttons | |
| ☆ ⤳ 9. | | | Didactic Displays | |
| ☆ ⤳ 10. | 29 | 0014 Botanical receptacle; 10... | Scientific Instruments | http://www.powerhousemuseum.com/collection/database/?irn=29 |
| ☆ ⤳ 11. | 35 | 002 1 coal-vase, Gloucester, ... | Coal boxes | http://www.powerhousemuseum.com/collection/database/?irn=35 |
| ☆ ⤳ 12. | | | Domestic Equipment-Home | |

A **row** is a single line of data in your dataset.

A **record** consists of all rows that belong to a single object. The first row of a record starts with non-null cells that identify the record; in subsequent rows, those identifying values are blank to indicate they belong to the same record.

While this avoids duplication of information and the errors that can occur because of that, it makes it difficult to see which categories belong to which object. For instance, if we create a text facet on **Categories** (see the previous recipe), we can click on each of the category names within the facet to see the rows that contain this category. However, if we do this, we will see a lot of empty rows:

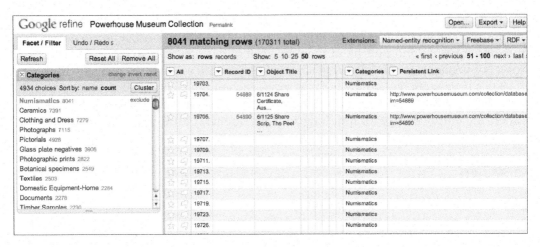

The reason for this is that OpenRefine indeed shows us all the rows where the category value is **Numismatics**, which includes the empty rows for all those objects where **Numismatics** was not the first category. However, it does not include the other rows that belong to the same object. This poses a problem if we are interested in all the rows of an object. For instance, we might want to star all objects in the **Numismatics** category so we can perform operations on them. Let's try this now and see what happens.

With **Numismatics** highlighted in the text facet, click on the **All** dropdown and navigate to **Edit rows | Star rows**. Now click on **reset** on the facet to see what has happened. We notice that only the rows with **Numismatics** in them are starred, but not the rows of the object to which these rows belong. Clearly we are missing something. So, let's undo the starring operation by reverting to the previous state from the **Undo / Redo** tab.

OpenRefine allows you to treat all rows that belong to the same object as a single **record**. That way, you have the benefits of splitting multi-valued cells to different rows while still being able to treat them as a whole. To switch to **records** mode, change the **Show as** setting on the top bar from **rows** to **records**. You will notice immediately that the alternate coloring scheme of OpenRefine changes. Instead of shading every other row, it now shades every other record, depending on the number of rows per record.

If we apply the **Numismatics** filter from the **Categories** facet now, while still in **records** mode, we see that all the fields of objects within the **Numismatics** category are selected instead. If we star those records using the **All** dropdown now, by navigating to **Edit rows | Star rows**, we see that all rows belonging to the object become starred:

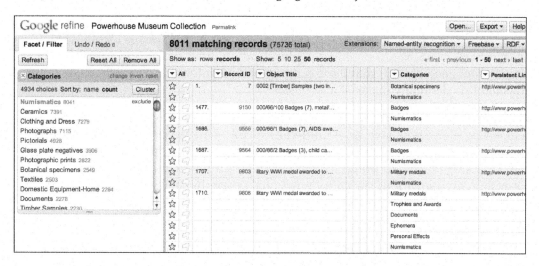

This indicates that, while in **records** mode, all operations happen on the entire record for which at least one row is matching. To summarize, we can say that **rows** mode shows you all individual rows that match your selection criteria, whereas **records** mode shows you all objects that have a matching row.

**Matching records that fit multiple criteria**

What if we want to match all records that are in the category **Numismatics** and also in the category **Medals**? To do this, we make sure that we are in **records** mode and we add a second text facet on the **Categories** field. In the first facet, we select **Numismatics**, and in the second facet, we select **Medals**. We now see all the records that are in both categories.

Now what happens if we switch back to **rows** mode? Suddenly, zero records are matching our selection. This seems strange at first, but it is actually pretty logical: no single row has a category which is equal to **Numismatics** and **Medals** at the same time; each row contains at most one of these two. Therefore, complex selections such as this one should be made in **records** mode.

Also, make sure you are back in **rows** mode for the other recipes in this book, or you might get totally unexpected results. If something inexplicable happens, always check first whether you are in the correct mode. This can save you a lot of headaches.

# Recipe 3 – clustering similar cells

Thanks to OpenRefine, you don't have to worry about inconsistencies that slipped in during the creation process of your data. If you have been investigating the various categories after splitting the multi-valued cells, you might have noticed that the same category labels do not always have the same spelling. For instance, there is `Agricultural Equipment` and `Agricultural equipment` (capitalization differences), `Costumes` and `Costume` (pluralization differences), and various other issues. The good news is that these can be resolved automatically; well, almost. But, OpenRefine definitely makes it a lot easier.

The process of finding the same items with slightly different spelling is called **clustering**. After you have split multi-valued cells, you can click on the **Categories** dropdown and navigate to **Edit cells | Cluster and edit...**. OpenRefine presents you with a dialog box where you can choose between different clustering methods, each of which can use various similarity functions. When the dialog opens, **key collision** and **fingerprint** have been chosen as default settings.

After some time (this can take a while, depending on the project size), OpenRefine will execute the clustering algorithm on the **Categories** field. It lists the found clusters in rows along with the spelling variations in each cluster and the proposed value for the whole cluster, as shown in the following screenshot:

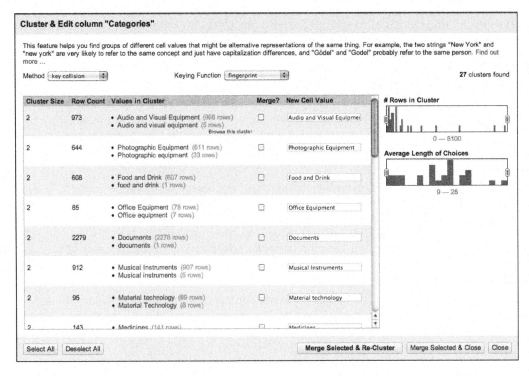

Note that OpenRefine does not automatically merge the values of the cluster. Instead, it wants you to confirm whether the values indeed point to the same concept. This avoids similar names, which still have a different meaning, accidentally ending up as the same.

Before we start making decisions, let's first understand what all of the columns mean. The **Cluster Size** column indicates how many different spellings of a certain concept were thought to be found. The **Row Count** column indicates how many rows contain either of the found spellings. In **Values in Cluster**, you can see the different spellings and how many rows contain a particular spelling. Furthermore, these spellings are clickable, so you can indicate which one is correct. If you hover over the spellings, a **Browse this cluster** link appears, which you can use to inspect all items in the cluster in a separate browser tab. The **Merge?** column contains a checkbox. If you check it, all values in that cluster will be changed to the value in the **New Cell Value** column when you click on one of the **Merge Selected** buttons. You can also manually choose a new cell value if the automatic value is not the best choice.

So, let's perform our first clustering operation. I strongly advise you to scroll carefully through the list to avoid clustering values that don't belong together. In this case, however, the algorithm hasn't acted too aggressively: in fact, all suggested clusters are correct. Instead of manually ticking the **Merge?** checkbox on every single one of them, we can just click on **Select All** at the bottom. Then, click on the **Merge Selected & Re-Cluster** button, which will merge all the selected clusters but won't close the window yet, so we can try other clustering algorithms as well.

OpenRefine immediately reclusters with the same algorithm, but no other clusters are found since we have merged all of them. Let's see what happens when we try a different similarity function. From the **Keying Function** menu, click on **ngram-fingerprint**. Note that we get an additional parameter, **Ngram Size**, which we can experiment with to obtain less or more aggressive clustering. We see that OpenRefine has found several clusters again. It might be tempting to click on the **Select All** button again, but remember we warned to carefully inspect all rows in the list. Can you spot the mistake? Have a closer look at the following screenshot:

| 2 | 12 | • Bookmarks (11 rows)<br>• book marks (1 rows) | ☐ | Bookmarks |
| 2 | 202 | • Shirts (115 rows)<br>• T-shirts (87 rows) | ☐ | Shirts |
| 2 | 3 | • Bonbon dishes (2 rows)<br>• Bon bon dishes (1 rows) | ☐ | Bonbon dishes |

Indeed, the clustering algorithm has decided that **Shirts** and **T-shirts** are similar enough to be merged. Unfortunately, this is not true. So, either manually select all correct suggestions, or deselect the ones that are not. Then, click on the **Merge Selected & Re-Cluster** button.

Apart from trying different similarity functions, we can also try totally different clustering methods. From the **Method** menu, click on **nearest neighbor**. We again see new clustering parameters appear (**Radius** and **Block Chars**, but we will use their default settings for now). OpenRefine again finds several clusters, but now, it has been a little too aggressive. In fact, several suggestions are wrong, such as the **Lockets / Pockets / Rockets** cluster. Some other suggestions, such as "Photocopiers" and "Photocopier", are fine. In this situation, it might be best to manually pick the few correct ones among the many incorrect clusters.

Assuming that all clusters have been identified, click on the **Merge Selected & Close** button, which will apply merging to the selected items and take you back into the main OpenRefine window. If you look at the data now or use a text facet on the **Categories** field, you will notice that the inconsistencies have disappeared.

**What are clustering methods?**

OpenRefine offers two different clustering methods, **key collision** and **nearest neighbor**, which fundamentally differ in how they function. With key collision, the idea is that a **keying function** is used to map a field value to a certain key. Values that are mapped to the same key are placed inside the same cluster. For instance, suppose we have a keying function which removes all spaces; then, A B C, AB C, and ABC will be mapped to the same key: ABC. In practice, the keying functions are constructed in a more sophisticated and helpful way.

Nearest neighbor, on the other hand, is a technique in which each unique value is compared to every other unique value using a **distance function**. For instance, if we count every modification as one unit, the distance between Boot and Bots is 2: one addition and one deletion. This corresponds to an actual distance function in OpenRefine, namely levenshtein.

In practice, it is hard to predict which combination of method and function is the best for a given field. Therefore, it is best to try out the various options, each time carefully inspecting whether the clustered values actually belong together. The OpenRefine interface helps you by putting the various options in the order they are most likely to help: for instance, trying key collision before nearest neighbor.

# Recipe 4 – transforming cell values

In *Chapter 2, Analyzing and Fixing Data*, we saw that OpenRefine can automatically change the contents of all cells in a column, such as trimming whitespace. In the previous recipe, we learned that clustering is another method to perform column-wide value changes. However, these operations are part of a more general mechanism for transforming cell contents. You can change the value of each cell in various complex ways. Although this looks a bit like Excel formulas, it is surprising to see how much can be done with just a little.

For instance, suppose you don't like the vertical bar as a separator in the **Categories** field and want to have a comma followed by a space instead. While this could be solved by first splitting the multi-valued cell and then joining it back together, we can do this actually in a single transformation step. Click on the **Categories** dropdown and navigate to **Edit cells | Transform...**. The transformation dialog appears as follows:

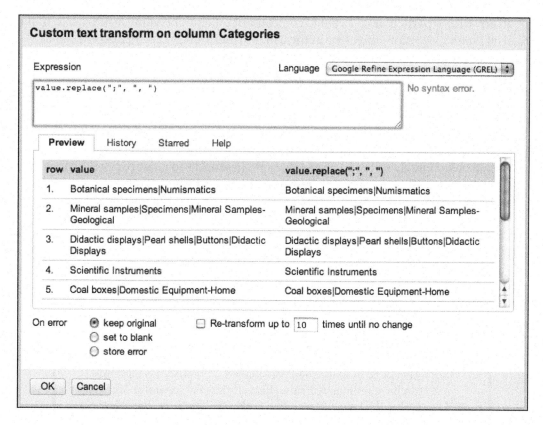

The heart of this dialog is **Expression,** a small script that explains OpenRefine how each of the values should change. The **Language** list allows us to choose the language for the expression, with current support for the **General Refine Expression Language (GREL)**, **Jython** (Python implemented in Java), and **Clojure** (a functional language that resembles Lisp). If you are familiar with the latter two, you might find it easier to write expressions in those languages. However, GREL was specifically created with simple transformations in mind, which is why we will use it in this book.

In the **Preview** tab, you see the values of the first few cells before and after the transformation. This allows you to iteratively change your transformation expression while seeing its result in real time. The **History** tab keeps track of expressions that you have used in the past, which is handy to recycle previous transformations. Expressions that you use a lot can be starred in the **History** tab, which makes them also appear in the **Starred** tab for even faster access. Finally, the **Help** tab gives an overview of the most important expression constructs.

At the bottom of the dialog, you can decide what happens if your expression results in an error for a particular cell value. You can opt to keep the value as it was, to make the cell blank, or to store the error in the cell. Furthermore, you can also choose to apply the transformation expression repeatedly, which can be useful if the result of the transformation is to be inspected again. For instance, if you have an expression that removes the first word that starts with a capital letter, you can repeat it until no words with capital letters are left.

Back to our mission: changing vertical bars into commas followed by a space. The default expression is `value`, but as you might have guessed, this is equivalent to the initial cell value. Let's try a simple example first and see what happens; so, enter `1234` as the new cell value. The preview is updated and shows that the new value of each cell will now be **1234**. Not very helpful, but you get the idea. What we actually want is to start from the original value and perform some replacements. In the **Help** tab, we can see that the corresponding GREL function for this is called `replace`. Since we want to replace vertical bars by commas, we enter the expression `value.replace("|", ", ")`. Note that we add quotation marks around the characters since they are strings, not numbers. The preview gets updated with the new cell values and the result is indeed what we expect, so we click on **OK**. In an amazingly short timespan, OpenRefine has transformed all cells in the **Categories** column, and all the vertical bars are now gone.

Always be careful when you change separators, because this can have unintended side-effects if the new separator occurs as part of the value. In fact, this is also the case here: the category **Cup, saucer and plate sets** contains a comma. So, if the field is to be processed again, this will likely cause mistakes. However, we will continue here with the comma for the sake of example.

To increase our confidence in cell transformations, we should probably try it again. Suppose we want to change semicolons into commas in the **Provenance** column. Click on the **Provenance (Production)** dropdown, **Edit cells**, **Transform…**, and type in the expression `value.replace(";", ",")`. The expression itself looks fine, but we see several error messages in the preview pane. This might be an opportunity to test the different **On error** settings (and I encourage you to do this), but we should actually reflect on what went wrong. The error messages read: **Error: replace expects 3 strings, or 1 string, 1 regex, and 1 string**; so somehow, our expression is passing the wrong input to `replace`. If we look at the values where this error message occurs, we see that `null` values are the culprit. Indeed, `null` is not a string, so we cannot replace characters inside of it. We need to tell OpenRefine that only non-empty cells must be transformed. Close the dialog by clicking on **Cancel**, click on the **Provenance (Production)** dropdown, and choose **Text filter**. Although we might have opted to select **Facet by blank**, we can save a little processing time by only transforming those cells that actually contain a semicolon. Enter `;` in the text filter, which will filter out all other values. Now retry the cell transformation and you will see that the transformation is only applied to the selected cells without causing any errors.

Finally, to show the power of cell transformations, we are going to do something really sophisticated. Although the vertical bars have now been changed into commas, there is still a problem with the **Categories** field. Indeed, several objects have the same category more than once, such as Record 14: **Didactic displays, Pearl shells, Buttons, Didactic displays**. Unfortunately, we cannot solve this the same way we eliminated duplicate rows before, because the duplicates here occur within one row. Luckily, GREL can help us. Open the transformation dialog on the **Categories** column and enter the following expression: `value.split(", ").uniques().join(", ")`. This expression looks complicated, but it is easy to understand the different parts: first, the value is split on every `,` (a comma followed by a space), then the unique values are retained with the `uniques` function, and finally they are joined back together. When you click on **OK**, OpenRefine will apply the transformation and inform you how many cells have been affected.

**Mastering GREL is easy**

This recipe introduced a few examples, but what if that doesn't fulfill your needs? *Appendix A, Regular Expressions and GREL* will introduce you to GREL so you can learn how to build expressions yourself.

# Recipe 5 – adding derived columns

Sometimes you do want to transform the contents of a cell, but also keep the original value. While you can go back to a cell's previous state using the **Undo / Redo** tab if something went wrong, it could be useful to see both the original value and the transformed value at the same time. Therefore, OpenRefine enables you to add a column based on another one.

Suppose we want to have a separate field that counts the number of categories per record. Click on the **Categories** dropdown, click on **Edit column** and **Add column based on this column...** A dialog very similar to the cell transformation dialog pops up; however, this time it additionally asks for a column name. Enter Category Count into the **New column name** field. Now, we have to create the expression that will count the number of categories. Since all categories are separated by a character (a vertical bar, or a comma if you followed the last recipe), we can simply split them and count the number of segments. This expression does the trick: value.split(",").length(). The **Preview** pane shows the result for the first view cells, and it looks alright, so click on **OK**.

OpenRefine has now created a new column. We can now use the **Category Count** column to analyze our data. For instance, we can create a facet by clicking on the **Category Count** dropdown and navigating to **Facet | Text facet**. Note that a text facet is easier here, even though the data is numeric, because we don't want to select ranges, but rather we want to inspect the individual counts. The facet appears on the left, informing us of how many objects have a specific number of categories assigned to them as shown in the following screenshot:

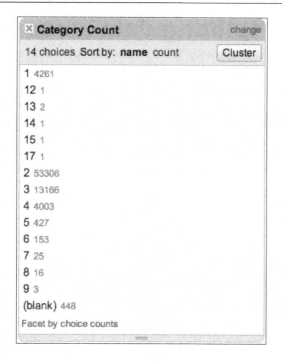

We also note something strange: one of the values is **(blank)**. If we click on it, we see that all corresponding records have an empty **Categories** field. Why doesn't the **Category Count** column just display that there are 0 categories? The answer is that for those empty cells, the transformation expression has resulted in an error because there was no value to split. As in the previous recipe, we could have filtered out those rows before we started the transformation. Instead, let's fix these rows. With the **(blank)** choice still highlighted in the facet, click on the **Category Count** column dropdown and navigate to **Edit cells | Transform…**. If we enter 0 as the expression and click on **OK**, the blank cells now contain 0. Don't be confused if you don't see any rows now: the **blank** filter is still active in the facet. Click on the **0** filter (or any other one) and you will see the data you expect.

From a data analysis standpoint, it is now interesting to see what numbers of categories per record are common. In the **Category Count** facet, set the **Sort by:** setting to **count**. We can now conclude that **2** categories per record is the most common case. Note that these numbers are all the more adequate if you have clustered the values and then removed duplicates, as indicated in the previous recipes. Once again, GREL has saved the day.

# Recipe 6 – splitting data across columns

We started this chapter by showing how you could split multiple values in a single cell across different rows. However, this might not always be what you want. In the examples so far, each of the different values had an identical role: one category is just like any other, and their order is interchangeable. The situation is different when a field is overloaded with different types of values. This can happen, for instance, when a `Clients` table contains a telephone field but no e-mail field and a contact person has provided both pieces of information. As a result, the person's telephone number and e-mail address could end up in the same field, separated by a slash.

We see a similar situation happen in various columns of the Powerhouse Museum Collection data. For instance, in the **Provenance** field, we see information about designers, makers, and various other things. It could be meaningful to put those in different columns so we can analyze them separately. To do this, click on the **Provenance (Production)** dropdown and navigate to **Edit column | Split into several columns...**. We then see a dialog with various splitting options:

**Split column Provenance (Production) into several columns**

**How to Split Column**

◉ by separator

    Separator | , | ☐ regular expression

    Split into [ ] columns at most (leave blank for no limit)

◯ by field lengths

    List of integers separated by commas, e.g., 5, 7, 15

**After Splitting**

☑ Guess cell type

☑ Remove this column

[ OK ] [ Cancel ]

We can chose between splitting **by separator**, which is what we have done so far, or **by field lengths**. The latter is meaningful if your field contains structured data such as `1987 en-us,X/Y`, where there are no fixed separators (or none at all). However, our data uses a simple separator. An interesting option is to set a limit, as there might otherwise be a lot of columns, so it might be wise to set it to something like 5. Don't forget to match the separator with the one of the data, which is the vertical bar | in our case. You can choose to let OpenRefine guess the cell type after the split (in case you have numeric values for instance) and to remove the original column.

After you click on **OK**, you will see that OpenRefine has replaced the one column called `Provenance (Production)` with several numbered columns called `Provenance (Production) 1`, `Provenance (Production) 2`, and so on, which can later be renamed according to the values they contain. Not all of the columns contain a value; values are found only in those records that had at least 5 items in the field. Although splitting will never create more columns than the limit you have set, it is possible that less columns are created if not as many values actually occur within a cell.

Another candidate for splitting is the **Object Title** column. We see that in some fields, the title is preceded by a number. It would prove interesting to split the number from the actual title. First, let's filter out the columns that start with a number. Click on the **Object Title** dropdown and click on **Text filter**. We need to write `starts with a number` in this field, which we can express with the regular expression `^\d`. This tells the filter to start at the beginning (`^`) and look for any digit (`\d`). Don't forget to tick the **regular expression** checkbox though, or OpenRefine will try to find that expression literally. We now only see titles that start with a number.

Click on the **Object Title** dropdown again and navigate to **Edit column | Split into several columns...**. We now use a single space as a separator, indicate that we want at most 2 columns, and then click on **OK**. The description number and title have moved to separate columns.

Splitting columns is far more powerful than splitting multi-valued cells as you have several configuration options. You can even use a regular expression to define the separator, which can then be different depending on the context. By the way, if this recipe made you curious about regular expressions, don't forget to check out *Appendix A, Regular Expressions and GREL*, which introduces them in more detail.

# Recipe 7 – transposing rows and columns

Sometimes data is not arranged into rows and columns the way you like. Indeed, there are different ways of arranging what belongs where, and the choices depend on the situation. In the Powerhouse Museum dataset, for instance, there are separate columns for several dimensions: `Height`, `Width`, `Depth`, `Diameter`, and `Weight`. However, not many objects have data for these columns, so the cost of maintaining them might be high with respect to the value they add. An alternative would be to transform these five columns into two columns: one that contains the name of the dimension (for instance, `Height` or `Weight`) and another that contains the measurement (for instance, `35mm` or `2kg`).

What we want to do here is to transpose the columns into rows. To do this, click on the **Height** dropdown and navigate to **Transpose | Transpose cells across columns into rows...**, which will bring up the following dialog:

On the left, you can choose from the **From Column**, the column from which to start the transposition. The **Height** column is already selected because we used it to bring up the transposition dialog. The **To Column** is where the transposition stops. The range between those two settings are the columns that will be transformed (so you have to bring them next to each other first, should they be separated). Here, we will select **Weight**, so those two columns and everything in between will be included in the transposition operation.

On the right-hand side, we can choose what will happen to the transposed columns. The first option, **Two new columns**, allows us to have one **Key column**, the one that will contain the original column name (Height, Weight...), and the **Value column**, which will contain the original cell values (35mm, 2kg...). You can choose the names for both columns, for instance, **Dimension** and **Measurement**. Alternatively, the **One column** option lets you merge the keys and values into a single cell; however, this can be more difficult to analyze later on. When the options have been set, click on **Transpose** to start the operation. The five columns are now rearranged into two as shown in the following screenshot:

| | | | Record ID | | | | Dimension | Measurement |
|---|---|---|---|---|---|---|---|---|

Show as: rows **records**     Show: 5 10 25 **50** records

| ▼ All | | | ▼ Record ID | | | | ▼ Dimension | ▼ Measurement |
|---|---|---|---|---|---|---|---|---|
| ☆ | 🖓 | 20. | 107 | | | | Height | 540 mm |
| ☆ | 🖓 | | | | | | Width | 350 mm |
| ☆ | 🖓 | | | | | | Depth | 300 mm |
| ☆ | 🖓 | 21. | 109 | | | | Height | 380 mm |
| ☆ | 🖓 | | | | | | Width | 520 mm |
| ☆ | 🖓 | 22. | 110 | | | | Height | 430 mm |
| ☆ | 🖓 | | | | | | Width | 200 mm |
| ☆ | 🖓 | | | | | | Depth | 150 mm |
| ☆ | 🖓 | 23. | 111 | | | | Height | 380 mm |
| ☆ | 🖓 | | | | | | Width | 230 mm |
| ☆ | 🖓 | | | | | | Depth | 240 mm |

Note how OpenRefine has again used records to keep related information together. So, if for a certain row different measurements were present, they have been spread across several rows. Maybe you would like to see all five values, even if some of them are empty. To achieve this, deselect the **Ignore blank cells** option in the transpose dialog.

Performing the reverse operation is also possible by navigating to the **Transpose | Columnize by key/value columns...** command. However, this operation is sensitive to blank cells, so proceed with caution. With some skill, you might be able to transform the **Provenance** columns which contain key/value pairs into full columns.

# Summary

This chapter has introduced recipes for advanced data operations. We have looked at multi-valued cells in different ways: when they had values of equal importance, we split them across several rows; when they had a different function, we split them across columns. We have also seen that OpenRefine has a special mode for working with multi-valued cells spread over different rows called **records** mode. In **records** mode, multiple rows that belong to the same object can be treated as one, giving you powerful search and manipulation options.

We also introduced you to clustering, which is really helpful if some of your cell values need to be consistent but are actually a bit messy. You can even go further and define your own transformation operations on cell values, and even create a new column based on an existing one. Finally, you have learned how to move data flexibly across rows and columns. Therefore, this chapter has given you access to the advanced possibilities offered by OpenRefine, which are hidden just a little deeper in the interface. By now, you can almost call yourself an OpenRefine master.

# 4
# Linking Datasets

Your dataset is not an island. Somewhere, related datasets exist, even in places where you might not expect them. For instance, if your dataset has a Country of Origin column, then it is related to a geographical database that lists the total area per country. An Author column in a book dataset relates to a list of authors with biographical data. All datasets have such connections, yet you might not know about them, and neither does the computer which contains your dataset. For instance, the record for `The Picture of Dorian Gray` might list `Wilde, O.` as its author, whereas a biographical dataset might only have an entry for `Oscar Wilde`. Even though they point to the same person, the string values are different, and it is thus difficult to connect the datasets. Furthermore, it would be really impractical to link all possible datasets to each other, as there are a huge number of them.

Instead, the approach is to find unique identifiers for cell values, and in particular, a **URL (Uniform Resource Locator)**. Instead of identifying Oscar Wilde by his name, we identify him with a URL such as `http://en.wikipedia.org/wiki/Oscar_Wilde`. Not only does this URL uniquely identify the writer Oscar Wilde (and not other people who happen to have the same name), it can also be visited in a browser to find more information about him, such as related datasets. Therefore, URLs allow us to connect different datasets together. In this chapter, we will learn methods to transform field values into URLs of the concepts they identify using the following recipes:

- Recipe 1 – reconciling values with Freebase
- Recipe 2 – installing extensions
- Recipe 3 – adding a reconciliation service
- Recipe 4 – reconciling with Linked Data
- Recipe 5 – extracting named entities

As usual, you can go straight to the recipe you're interested in. However, be sure to learn how to install OpenRefine extensions first before you continue to the last three recipes. Every recipe starts from the cleaned Powerhouse Museum dataset, in which the **Categories** column has been spread across several rows.

# Recipe 1 – reconciling values with Freebase

When you want to transform your cell values from simple strings to URLs, different choices are possible. After all, a given concept can be identified with many URLs as there are many pages on the Web about the same topic. This need not be a problem as long as each URL unambiguously identifies a single concept. However, we must choose which URL we want to use. On the Web, there are many databases of concepts, the most well-known being Wikipedia. In addition to databases for humans, there are also several databases targeted at machines. One example is Freebase, a collaborative knowledge base in which machine-readable facts about virtually every topic are stored.

> Before OpenRefine was called Google Refine, it was owned by Freebase creator *MetaWeb* and called **Freebase Gridworks**. As a tool for manipulating large datasets, it fitted nicely in the Freebase philosophy of making structured data available.

Therefore, we will reconcile our cell values with Freebase URLs. Since Freebase reconciliation is built in OpenRefine, we can try it right away. Note that we're starting from the Powerhouse dataset in which the **Categories** column has been split across rows. This is important, as each cell should contain a single value that matches a Freebase topic. A full-text field such as **Description** is thus not a good candidate for reconciliation (it is, however, a good candidate for named-entity extraction, as you can see in the last recipe of this chapter).

To start reconciliation, go to the **Categories** dropdown and navigate to **Reconcile | Start reconciling…**. OpenRefine shows the reconciliation dialog. On the right side of the dialog, you see all possible reconciliation services. Two Freebase reconciliation services are built-in:

- **Freebase Query-based Reconciliation**: This is useful if your column values are already Freebase IDs (such as `/en/solar_system`) or GUIDs (hexadecimal identifiers).
- **Freebase Reconciliation Service**: This offers a more general approach for terms that are not necessarily related to Freebase identifiers.

Clearly we are in the second case here, so select **Freebase Reconciliation Service**. After some processing, OpenRefine loads the options of this service on the right-hand side:

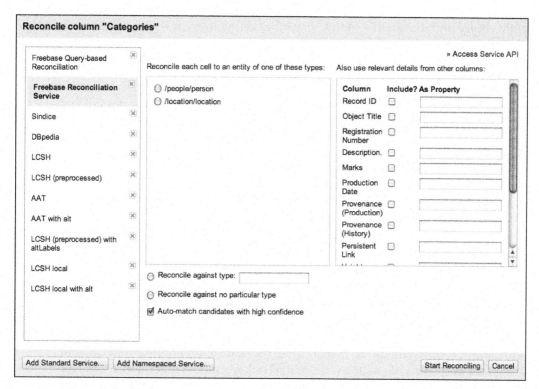

 The services in your OpenRefine installation might be different from the ones you see in the screenshot. That's because you can add reconciliation services yourself, as we'll show you in one of the next recipes.

There are three options you can set now. First, you have to decide against what type of records you want to reconcile. This can restrict the search to specific topics, which is handy if your column contains only city or person names for instance. This way, reconciliation can happen faster, and there is a lower chance of finding a false positive. During the processing step after you have selected the service, OpenRefine has contacted the service with part of your data to try to guess the type of your column data. Unfortunately for us, it offers two options that are not relevant to the **Categories** field: persons and locations. Luckily, we also have the option to choose a type ourselves with **Reconcile against type**. However, as we're not sure whether the categories in our dataset actually belong to a single specific type, we just select **Reconcile against no particular type**.

The second option we can choose is **Auto-match candidates with high confidence**. Reconciliation services also return a match score that indicate how confident they are that the match is the right one. The auto-match option is on by default, and it means that if the score is sufficiently high, OpenRefine will assume it has made the right choice and declare it a match. For other cell values (or if you have unticked the checkbox), you will have to confirm the match manually. Our advice would be to leave this one ticked, as it saves you a considerable amount of work.

The third and final option allows you to send additional data to the reconciliation service. Instead of basing the match on a single column value, it is possible to consider different columns. For this, you will have to indicate the property name. For the Powerhouse Museum dataset, no such other relevant column exists. But if you had a dataset of country names with country codes, it could be helpful to send both to the reconciliation service.

With **Reconcile against no particular type** ticked, click on **Start Reconciling**. The reconciliation process might take some time, as OpenRefine will now ask the reconciliation service to find a URL for each unique cell value. The yellow information bar on top of the window will tell you how much has been done.

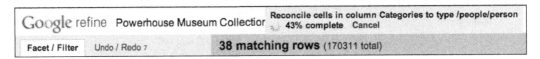

This might be the moment to take a coffee break or to do another task on your computer and let reconciliation run in the background. When the process has finished, you will notice that OpenRefine has automatically created a **judgement** and a **best candidate's score** facet for you.

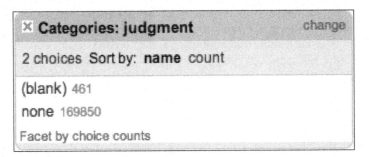

The **judgement** facet allows you to partition the dataset in rows that have been reconciled and rows that have not, as well as rows that have a blank value for the **Categories** cell and were thus not reconciliation candidates. What you see here might surprise you, there are only **(blank)** and **none** filters in the facet. Where are the reconciled rows?

It turns out that, unfortunately, reconciliation with Freebase has not been successful no single match was found. Does this mean we did something wrong? No, we did not, it just happens that the terms in our database are apparently not the kind of topics that Freebase covers. Does that mean that Freebase is not a good candidate for reconciliation? Not at all, it just so happens that our dataset is not a good fit. You might have more luck with other datasets, so definitely try that.

Let's undo the unsuccessful reconciliation by removing the facets with the **Remove All** button and by going a step back in the **Undo / Redo** menu. (You can get them back by going to the **Categories** dropdown | **Reconcile** | **Facets**.) The next recipes will show you how to try other reconciliation services.

Sometimes you just want to try out reconciliation with a certain service to see how it works. Does that mean you have to sit through the whole reconciliation process every time? Not if you make clever use of facets! We tend to try reconciliation first on a small part of the dataset and then decide whether we want to run it on all rows. To make a more or less random selection, we can for instance add a text filter on the **Record ID** column and enter a digit such as 4. Given an equal distribution of digits in all IDs, this would select about 10 percent of the rows. If that's still too much, just keep adding digits until the number of rows has come down to a few hundred. For instance, 413 did the trick for us.

# Recipe 2 – installing extensions

While OpenRefine allows you out-of-the-box to add new reconciliation services, these are only services that work in a certain way under the hood. However, there are several other types of services out there, and if you want to use them, you will need to add some functionality to OpenRefine in the form of extensions. So, before we can show you how to add those services, we first have to explain how to install OpenRefine extensions. Not all extensions offer reconciliation services, so this recipe describes the general installation procedure. At the time of writing, several OpenRefine extensions are available, including the following points:

- The RDF extension by **Digital Enterprise Research Institute (DERI)**, which adds support for RDF export and reconciliation with SPARQL endpoints. We'll explain both terms in the next recipe.

- The **Named-Entity Recognition (NER)** extension written by one of the authors of this book, which allows you to extract URLs from full-text fields. Usage of this extension is covered in detail in the last recipe of this chapter.

Like OpenRefine, all extensions are available freely. An up-to-date list of available extensions is maintained at `https://github.com/OpenRefine/OpenRefine/wiki/Extensions`, which also includes their download locations. As the extensions are very diverse, it might look tricky to install them. However, this recipe will show you the technique to install any extension.

First, you will have to find the path where extensions need to be installed. This depends on your operating system, but OpenRefine can help you find it. At the bottom of the starting page, there is a link called **Browse workspace directory**.

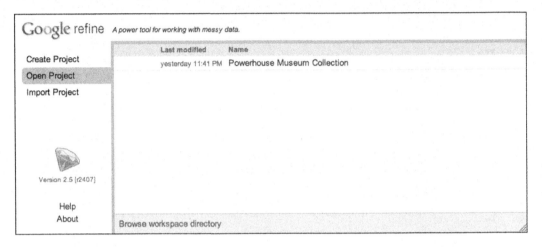

If you click on this link, you will end up in the OpenRefine application folder (at least on Windows and Mac; for Linux, read on). In this folder, you have to create a new folder called `extensions` if it doesn't exist yet. This will be the path in which you need to add the extensions. For the different operating systems, it should look like the following points:

- **Windows**: `C:\Documents and Settings\(your username)\Application Data\OpenRefine\extensions` or possibly in the `Local Settings` folder instead at `C:\Documents and Settings\(your username)\Local Settings\Application Data\OpenRefine\extensions`

- **Mac OS X**: `/Users/(your username)/Library/Application Support/OpenRefine/extensions` or, starting from your home folder, in `/Users/(your username)/Library/Application Support/OpenRefine/extensions`

- **Linux**: `/home/refine/webapp/extensions`

The next step is to download an extension and to place it in the folder. For instance, let's install the RDF extension. Download the extension from `http://refine.deri.ie/`; this will get you a ZIP file in your downloads folder. Unpack the contents of this ZIP archive in the way you're used to. Depending on the software you use, additional folders might be generated, but the folder we are interested in is called `rdf-extension`.

Move this folder to the OpenRefine's `extensions` folder we found earlier. In the `extensions` folder, you should now see a folder called `rdf-extension`, which in turn contains other folders, such as `images`, `MOD-INF`, `scripts`, and `styles`.

Now restart OpenRefine to make the extension active. Just closing the browser window is not enough; you have to actually close the OpenRefine application itself by right or control-clicking on its icon on the bottom of your screen and choosing **Close**. Then, start OpenRefine again as usual and open a project. When the project has loaded, a new RDF button in the top-right tells you that the installation has been successful:

If you don't see the button, make sure that the right extension folder has been placed in the correct location and that OpenRefine has been properly restarted.

You can repeat the steps in this recipe for other extensions as well. In the next recipes, we will use the RDF extension, so make sure to install it. In a later recipe, we will also need the NER extension, so you should install that as well while you're at it.

# Recipe 3 – adding a reconciliation service

For this recipe, you need to have installed the RDF extension. If you didn't, have a look at the previous recipe. If you did, you might wonder what the terms RDF and SPARQL mean, as they are used throughout this extension. This will become clear right now.

The **Resource Description Framework (RDF)** is a model for data that can be interpreted by machines. While humans can read HTML on the Web, machines do not understand natural language and must therefore be given information in another form. Disambiguation is an important aspect; does Washington refer to the city or the person? And which person? To express this, information in RDF is referred to by URIs or URLs, just like we do with reconciliation in OpenRefine. This is why RDF comes in handy for reconciliation.

The **SPARQL Protocol and RDF Query Language** (a recursive acronym for **SPARQL**) is a language for querying RDF datasources. Traditional relational databases use SQL as a query language; RDF databases and important for us, reconciliation services, communicate in SPARQL.

If you want to reconcile your data with an RDF datasource, then you must tell OpenRefine how it must communicate with this datasource. When you installed the RDF extension, you already added support for SPARQL to OpenRefine. However, before we can reconcile our cell values to URLs, we must configure the datasource. To do this, click on the new RDF button in the top-right and navigate to **Add reconciliation service | Based on SPARQL endpoint...**. Note that you can also reconcile with a local RDF file, which is handy if you have your own dataset of URLs. OpenRefine shows you the **Add SPARQL-based reconciliation service** dialog.

This dialog allows you to choose a name for the SPARQL endpoint, to add the endpoint's details (where it is located and how it works), and what kind of information is used to match the cell value to a URL. You can use a SPARQL endpoint of your own or any of the publicly available endpoints listed at `http://www.w3.org/wiki/SparqlEndpoints`.

For this example, we will use an endpoint that we have set up. It includes a processed version of the publicly available **Library of Congress Subject Headings (LCSH)** dataset. To use this endpoint, fill out the details as follows:

- **Name**: `LCSH`
- **Endpoint URL**: `http://sparql.freeyourmetadata.org/`
- **Graph URI**: `http://sparql.freeyourmetadata.org/authorities-processed/`
- **Type**: **Virtuoso**
- **Label properties**: tick only **skos:prefLabel**

The **Endpoint URL** is the address where the endpoint is located, and the **Graph URI** identifies which dataset within this endpoint should be used. The **Type** of the endpoint is used to indicate the underlying endpoint software; it is not mandatory to specify this, but knowing the correct type enables low-level tricks that greatly improve the reconciliation speed. Finally, the **Label properties** indicate names of fields that can be used to look up the cell value. In RDF, these properties usually have common names (which are in fact mostly URLs themselves). Once these properties have been set, click on the **OK** button.

As nothing happens right now, you might be curious to know how you can check whether the new reconciliation has been added properly. You can verify this by bringing up the reconciliation dialog by going to the **Categories** dropdown and navigating to **Reconcile | Start reconciling...**. On the left-hand side, you will see the newly added service. Now read on to the next recipe if you can't wait to start using it!

# Recipe 4 – reconciling with Linked Data

In the previous recipe, we talked about RDF and SPARQL without sketching the broader context in which these technologies were created, so let's introduce them now. Around the year 2000, web researchers and engineers were noticing that humans were no longer the only consumers of the Web; more and more machine clients, and thus pieces of software, started using the Web for various purposes. However, every such piece of software had to be hardcoded for a particular task, and they could not parse the natural language in documents on the human Web. Therefore, a vision called the **Semantic Web** was coined, a Web in which information would also be interpretable for machines. This was the start of RDF and SPARQL.

However, the vision was rather abstract and difficult to many people. Several of the concepts relied on concepts such as ontologies and reasoning, which can become very complex rapidly. *Tim Berners-Lee*, inventor of the Web and one of the creators of the Semantic Web vision, realized this and launched the Linked Data principles (`http://www.w3.org/DesignIssues/LinkedData.html`). These principles shifted the focus of the Semantic Web to the creation of data that was interlinked with other datasets. The principles are as follows:

1. Use URIs as names for things
2. Use HTTP URIs so that people can look up those names
3. When someone looks up a URI, provide useful information using the standards (RDF, SPARQL)
4. Include links to other URIs so that they can discover more things

So, the first principle asks to use unambiguous identifiers for your concepts and the second principle asks specifically for HTTP URIs, which are thus URLs. These principles have been used in the datasets we will use for reconciliation. The third principle is concerned with how your data is published. In fact, the RDF extension allows us to export our dataset as RDF, so that's covered as well. The fourth principle is about linking to other datasets, which is exactly what reconciliation will do for us.

Without further ado, let's start reconciliation. Like in *Recipe 1 – reconciling values with Freebase*, go to the **Categories** dropdown and navigate to **Reconcile | Start reconciling...**, which will bring up the reconciliation dialog on your screen. This time, however, select the **LCSH reconciliation service** from the left-hand side which you installed in the previous recipe. OpenRefine will now try out some of the cell values to see if it can determine its type. After a few seconds, it suggests that the values have type `skos:Concept`. This is indeed true, as all **Category** values are in fact concepts. You can leave all settings as they are and click on **Start Reconciling**.

 As indicated previously, you might want to try this on a subset of the dataset to avoid a long waiting time. Or, you can get a cup of tea now.

When the reconciliation is done, you will notice three things. First, OpenRefine has created the two facets that help us find matched and unmatched rows. Second, you see a green bar on top of the **Category** column, which indicates how many of the cell values have been reconciled. Third, the cell values are displayed differently; some of them are in blue and others have new options.

| ▼ All | ▼ Record ID | ▼ Object Title | | ▼ Categories |
|---|---|---|---|---|
| ☆ ◻ 164. | 724 | 1062 Column, dark Devonshire marble, quarried near Torquay, Devon, England, purchased 1883 | | Columns |
| ☆ ◻ | | | | Choose new match |
| | | | | Stones |
| | | | | ☑ ☑ Stones River (Tenn.) (0.3) |
| | | | | ☑ ☑ Stones River Watershed (Tenn.) (0.2) |
| | | | | ☑ ☑ Stones River National Battlefield (Tenn.) (0.146) |
| | | | | ☑ ☑ Create new topic |
| | | | | Search for match |
| | | | | Mineral Samples-Geological |
| | | | | ☑ ☑ Create new topic |
| ☆ ◻ | | | | Search for match |
| | | | | Specimens |
| ☆ ◻ | | | | Choose new match |

Let's first focus on the reconciled values displayed in blue. The more of them you see, the more successful the reconciliation has been (and thus, the greener the bar on top of the column will be). They are blue because they are in fact links; if you click on them, you end up on the page with the URL the term has been reconciled to. For instance, if we click on the **Specimens** link, we are directed towards `http://id.loc.gov/authorities/subjects/sh87006764.html`, which is indeed the entry for Specimens in the Library of Congress Subject Headings. So this is how we create Linked Data; instead of just the string `Specimens`, which looks like nine random characters to a computer, OpenRefine reconciled the value with a URL. This URL can be interpreted by a machine, as that URL in turn links to other URLs that help define its meaning.

When you see unreconciled values in black, you have not been so lucky for this particular term. They are not links, so OpenRefine has not been able to find a matching URL automatically. There are two cases of unreconciled values; first, those where some suggestions have been found, but OpenRefine was not able to find the right one. In that case, it will list several alternatives for you. If any of those alternatives is correct, you can either click on the single checkmark, which will replace only the current cell value by the chosen term, or the double checkmark, which will replace all cells that have the same value. Be careful when replacing all identical values though, as some might actually refer to another term. Note that you can also click on the suggestions, which will bring you to their corresponding web page for more information.

The other case with unreconciled values is when OpenRefine did not find any suggestions. In that case, you're out of luck. Maybe the term in question does not exist in the dataset you're reconciling against, or maybe it is named differently. In any case, the only thing you can do is assign a URL manually. To do this, click on the **search for match** link, which will show you a dialog that helps with finding the correct match.

A final option is to create a new topic for the cell value by clicking on the **Create new topic** link, or by choosing the **New Topic** button from the **Search for Match** dialog. This will not create a new URL in the LCSH dataset (as you don't have the permission to do that), but it will mark the cell value as **new**. This will enable you to select all those cells in the **judgement** facet so you will be able to do something else with them. For instance, you could reconcile all new values with another dataset to see if you find matches there.

You'll probably wonder how you can get the URLs that reconciliation has brought us. Yet, at the same time, we still want to keep the original category names. So, the right way to do this would be to create a new column based on the **Categories** column as we've done before. Click on the **Categories** dropdown and navigate to **Edit Column | Add column based on this column....** We will call this column `Category URLs`. The expression that transforms the reconciled cell to its URL is `cell.recon.match.id`. This piece of GREL selects the cell, takes its reconciliation information, gets out the accepted reconciliation match, and extracts the ID (the URL in this case). The cells that do not have a match will result in an error, so make sure that for error, the **set to blank** option is chosen. After clicking on **OK**, you will see a new column with the corresponding URLs.

When you're done with the reconciliation process and have extracted the URLs that you need, you might want to give the **Categories** column back its old appearance. After all, the reconciliation data is still there and this can be distracting. To clear it, go to the **Categories** dropdown one more time, navigating to **Reconcile | Actions | Clear reconciliation data**. The categories column is now a regular column again. Additionally, you can remove the facets by clicking on **Remove All** on top of the left sidebar.

# Recipe 5 – extracting named entities

Reconciliation works great for those fields in your dataset that contain single terms, such as names of people, countries, or works of art. However, if your column contains running text, then reconciliation cannot help you, since it can only search for single terms in the datasets it uses. Fortunately, another technique called `named-entity extraction` can help us. An extraction algorithm searches texts for named entities which are text elements, such as names of persons, locations, values, organizations, and other widely-known things. In addition to just extracting the terms, most algorithms also try to perform disambiguation. For instance, if the algorithm finds Washington in a text, it will try to determine whether the city or the person is mentioned. This saves us from having to perform reconciliation on the extracted terms.

OpenRefine does not support named-entity recognition natively, but the Named-Entity Recognition extension adds this for you. Before continuing with this recipe, download the extension from `http://software.freeyourmetadata.org/ner-extension/` and follow the *Installing extensions* recipe. If the installation was successful, you are greeted by the **Named-entity recognition** button in the top-right of your screen after restarting OpenRefine.

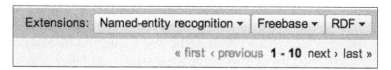

 For this recipe, you might want to start from the dataset where the categories have not been split over several rows, as named-entity recognition will create new rows if multiple terms have been found for a single record. That can become confusing if you already have multiple rows per record.

Looking at the Powerhouse Museum dataset, we see that the **Descriptions** column is a good candidate for named-entity extraction as it contains running text. If we want to link this field to other datasets, we must extract entities first. To do this, click on the **Descriptions** dropdown and choose **Extract named entities...** at the bottom. The **Extract named entities** dialog appears on your screen.

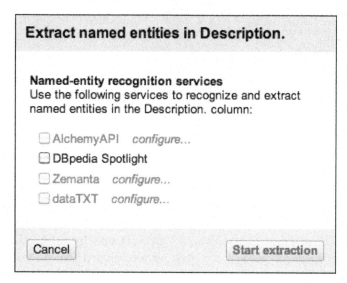

The extension itself does not contain any named-entity recognition algorithms but uses existing services instead, just like the reconciliation functionality also relies on external reconciliation services. This allows you to choose the services that you prefer. However, in contrast with the reconciliation services, which are open, some of the named-entity recognition services require that you create an account. While all supported services have a free option, some of them also offer premium accounts that give you additional benefits, such as faster or unlimited extraction.

The DBpedia Spotlight service does not require an account, and is thus already available. Therefore, tick on its checkbox in the dialog and choose **Start extraction**. OpenRefine will now start the extraction process, which can take some time. Therefore, as we explained before, it might be interesting to try the extraction on a subset first. Premium services might offer faster extraction. However, if you tick on multiple checkboxes to perform the extraction with multiple services at once, the extraction is only as fast as the slowest service.

When named-entity recognition has finished, you see that OpenRefine has created a new column next to the **Description** column called **DBpedia Spotlight**.

| Show as: rows **records**     Show: 5 10 25 **50** records | | « first ‹ previous **1** ‑ |
|---|---|---|
| ▼ **Record ID** | ▼ **Description.** | ▼ **DBpedia Spotlight** |
| 162 | Building stone, Cunliffe, [Yorkshire / Derbyshire / Cumbria], England, purchased in 1883. A very fine-grained hard sandstone from the lower Millstone-grit series. Its great density and homogeneous character bespeak it as suitable for steps and landings where there is great wear. Blocks of almost any size can be obtained. It was chosen for the International Exhibition at South Kensington. | Millstone<br>Choose new match |
| | | grit<br>Choose new match |
| 173 | Building stone, Derbyshire Grit, quarried at Whatslandwell, Derbyshire, England, purchased 1883 Building stone, Derbyshire Grit. This is a purple-grey stone. It belongs to the carboniferous series and is much used for all classes of engineering work. Locality: Whatslandwell, Derbyshire. | |
| 184 | Building stone, Darley Dale, quarried at Darley Dale, near <atlock, Derbyshire, England, purchased 1883. A light ferruginous brown sandstone belonging to the carboniferous series. Its weight is 148 lbs per cubic ft. The colums of Leeds Town Hall and the whole of the front of St George's Hall, Liverpool, are made of this stone. Locality: Darley Dale near Matlock, Derbyshire. | Leeds Town Hall<br>Choose new match |

In this new column, you see the extracted terms. If multiple terms were found, they are split across several rows, so you can switch between the rows and records modes of OpenRefine. The screenshot shows that **DBpedia Spotlight** found two terms in record **162**, no terms in record **173**, and one term in record **184**. As you can see, the terms are displayed in blue, indicating that they are in fact links. For instance, if you click on **Leeds Town Hall**, you arrive at a page about this building with links to related resources. This is Linked Data at its best; what used to be a human-only text field now has machine-interpretable links to the concepts it contains.

However, you might be disappointed to see that not all cell values have associated terms. So, let's see if other services do a better job. For that, we have to add our account information for each of those services. To do this, click on the **Named-entity recognition** button in the top-right and choose **Configure API keys....** The following dialog shows you the supported services and the configuration parameters they require:

## Configuration — Named-Entity Recognition Extension

### Services

**AlchemyAPI** *configuration instructions*

API key

**DBpedia Spotlight**

Confidence  0.5

Support  30

**Zemanta** *configuration instructions*

API key

**dataTXT** *configuration instructions*

App ID

App key

Language  en

Confidence  0.1

Epsilon  0.3

Text
Chunks

Cancel                                                    **Update**

For instance, if you want to perform named-entity recognition with **Zemanta**, add your **Application programming interface** (**API**) key to the corresponding field. If you don't have an API key yet, click on the **configuration instructions** link. This will take you to a page that lists the steps to obtain an API key with **Zemanta**. All services have a free option, so you can just register for an account to try out the service on your data. In addition to that, some services can be configured with additional parameters that determine the service's functionality. The configuration instructions can be very helpful here.

When you have configured additional services and have tried named-entity extraction on the **Description** column again, you will now be able to select multiple services at once. The results of each separate service will be added to a new column, so you could have additional **Zemanta** and **AlchemyAPI** columns, each of which will contain extracted terms. Depending on the dataset, you might have more success with one service or another, so be sure to experiment!

# Summary

In this chapter, we have seen how your dataset can be transformed from an isolated island into a connected collection of data. On one hand, you can perform reconciliation on columns that contain simple field values. Therefore, the text in the cells is given meaning by adding a URL to it which can be looked up online. You can either use the built-in Freebase reconciliation or install the RDF extension which allows reconciliation against Linked Data sources. On the other hand, you can perform named-entity recognition on cells that contain flowing text, again with an extension. This lets OpenRefine search for concepts inside the cell values, and it will try to find a URL for each of them. In the end, your dataset becomes enriched with links to other datasets, which is a valuable asset when you're publishing your dataset on the Web.

# Regular Expressions and GREL

Two more utilities are available in the advanced OpenRefine user's toolbox: regular expressions and GREL. **Regular expressions** are patterns for matching and replacing text that come in very handy when dealing with large quantities of data. The **General Refine Expression Language**, **GREL**, gives you access to a bit of programming power for those cases where a specialized manipulation is necessary. This appendix will introduce you to both techniques.

## Regular expressions for text patterns

OpenRefine offers many ways to find the data you need. But what if you don't know the exact text, or more commonly with large datasets, what if the text slightly varies from cell-to-cell? While finding all cells with a value that contains the letter a is easy, finding values that contain a number (or worse, the letter a followed by a number) is more difficult. This is where regular expressions come in handy.

The purpose of a regular expression is to define a pattern of text instead of a precise chunk of text. It allows you to say things such as "a letter followed by a number" and many more complex things. Regular expressions are built from **character classes** that represent the characters you are looking for woven together by **quantifiers**, **anchors**, **choices**, and **groups**.

OpenRefine allows you to try out regular expressions in an easy way. Create a text filter on any column (the **Object Title** column in the Powerhouse Museum dataset is especially interesting) by clicking on its dropdown and choosing **Text filter**. In the newly created filter, tick the **regular expression** checkbox and you're ready to go (refer to the following screenshot). The data will now be filtered according to the expression you enter:

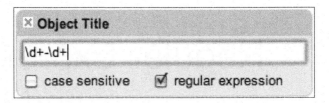

# Character classes

Regular expressions use **character classes** (letters, numbers, whitespace) as an indication for the character you are looking for. For instance, if you are looking for letters or numbers, you can type them directly:

- The pattern `Aar` will look for all texts that contain a capital A followed by a small a and r. If the **case sensitive** box is not ticked, the capitalization will not matter.

- The pattern `123` finds all texts that contain this number. Note that texts with the number `41235` are also matched, since `123` is a textual part of that.

- As you can see, this does not differ from regular text matching yet. With regular expressions, we can also say that we expect any letter or any number. We can give a **set of characters** from which can be chosen by surrounding the alternatives with square brackets `[]`. We can indicate a **character range** in those brackets by separating the limits with a hyphen.

- The pattern `[0123456789]` matches all texts that contain a number.

- The pattern `[0-9]` does the same, only it is more condense. It says everything between 0 and 9 is fine.

- Similarly, the pattern `[a-z]` matches all lowercase letters (and also uppercase if the case-sensitive option is not used). `[A-Z]` matches uppercase letters and `[a-zA-Z]` matches all letters, regardless of the case-sensitive option.

- If you want to look for numbers and letters, use `[0-9a-zA-Z]`. Read this as "every character between 0 and 9, between a and z, or between A and Z".

- As in the earlier examples, we can put several matchers next to each other. `analy[sz]e` will match both American (analyze) and British (analyse) spellings.

- Similarly, the expression [0-9] [a-z] will find numbers directly followed by at least one letter. The expression [a-z] [0-9] [0-9] [0-9] finds letters directly followed by at least three numbers.

- If you want to find measurements such as 1 cm or 25 in, you will not find them with the preceding expressions because of the space in between. Luckily, a space is also a symbol, so the expression [0-9] [a-z] will find them. Note the space in between the bracket pairs, and note the fact that this will even find longer measurements such as 12345 meters. Indeed, the expression matches a number followed by a space and a letter, so in this case, 5 m. It doesn't matter whether other numbers or letters are also present.

- If you're just looking for measurements in inches, the expression [0-9] in will do the job.

- It might be a bit cumbersome to write [0-9] in full every time. This is why **shorthand character classes** were introduced. They are symbols that stand for a set of characters. For instance, the symbol \d stands for any digit and is thus equivalent to [0-9], but a lot faster to write. The opposite is \D, which means anything that is not a digit and includes letters as well as symbols. Unfortunately, there is no shorthand for any letter, but there is a shorthand for any letter, number, or underscore, which is \w, which stands for any word character. Again, the opposite is \W, which matches for all non-letters and non-numbers that are not underscores either.

- \d [a-z] will again match for texts with measurements: any number followed by a space and a letter.

- \d\d\d matches texts with numbers with a length of at least three.

- \D\D matches texts that have at least two consecutive non-numbers. If you're surprised to see texts with numbers as well, think about it: the expression only says that the text should contain a non-number followed by a non-number; it doesn't say that there should be no numbers at all. However, if a text field only contains numbers, it won't be matched. To rephrase, the expression means "I'm looking for two non-numbers in a row, do you have them?"

- You might wonder how \D works. Does it then translate to a huge set that includes everything but numbers? The answer is more simple: using a caret ^ as the first character in braces means none of the characters should be present in the pattern. Therefore, \D stands for [^0-9].

- The expression [^a-zA-Z0-9] looks for texts that contain something which is not a letter or number. Most texts will match, as for instance spaces and punctuation marks are still allowed. However, empty fields will not match, as there must be at least one character which is not a letter or number.

- The expression `[^a-zA-Z0-9]\d[^a-zA-Z0-9]` means any digit surrounded by non-letters or non-numbers. For instance, we see that single digits in parentheses are matched. Note that items such as `(123)` will not be matched, but `(3)` will, as we explicitly say that it should be a single digit.

If you really want to match any character, the dot `.` is what you need. This symbol matches anything (except newlines, which are `\n`). While that might not seem useful by itself, it is very useful when combined with other character classes:

- The pattern `a.a.a` matches any text where an `a` is followed by any character, another `a`, any character, and another `a`. For instance, texts with the words `dulcamara`, `alabaster`, and `salamander` will match.

- The pattern `19..` (there is a space before and after) will match years in the 20th century.

- However, you should be careful with the dot: the last pattern also matches `19th` and `19M$`, because a dot really means anything. If a year is what you want, `19\d\d` is more accurate.

Now, you might wonder what to do if you want to match an actual dot, actual square brackets, or an actual backslash followed by a "d". The trick is to tell in the regular expression when you don't want a symbol to be recognized as something special. For letters, numbers, spaces, and a few other characters, this is the default. Characters that have a special meaning need to be escaped by preceding them with a backslash `\`. A literal dot is thus represented as `\.`; the backslash itself as `\\`.

- To find texts that have three consecutive dots in them, use `\.\.\.` (This can actually be done in a more handy way, as we'll see in the next section.)

- To find texts with a backslash, use `\\`. (There are none in the dataset.)

- Texts that contain an opening or a closing square bracket are found with `[\[\]]`. This looks complicated, but it is quite logical: the first and last bracket say "choose any of the things within". And the things within are actual square brackets, but they have to be escaped, so they become `\[` and `\]`.

- With `[2]`, you find texts that contain the number 2 ("choose any of the things within", and the only thing within is a 2). With `\[2\]`, you find texts with the number 2 surrounded in square brackets, as the brackets are escaped this time and thus have no special meaning anymore.

# Quantifiers

So far, we've seen ways in regular expressions to indicate that we want to encounter certain characters. However, we cannot yet express if we want to see characters a certain number of times without this number being known in advance. For instance, how can we say "a number within single quotes"? We could start with `'\d'`, but that would show us only texts that contain 0, 1, 5, and so on, but not multidigit numbers such as 23 or 478. Indeed, computers follow the expression slavishly: one single quote, one digit, one single quote.

**Quantifiers** can express repetition. There are three simple quantifiers: a plus sign `+`, which means one or more times, an asterisk `*`, which means zero or more times, and a question mark `?`, which means zero or one time. They only exert an effect on the symbol that is directly to the left of them:

- `bre+d` matches texts that contain `bred`, `breed`, or `breeed` with any number of `e`, as long as at least one `e` is present.

- `bre*d` matches texts that contain `brd`, `bred`, `breed`, or `breeed` with any number of `e`, even without. Note how `brd` is matched with the asterisk, but not with the plus sign.

- `bre?d` matches `brd` and `bred`, but not `breed` or any other number of `es`. Put simply, it makes the `e` optional.

- Combinations are also possible. `br?e+d` matches `bed`, `bred`, `beed`, `breed`, `beeed`, `breeed`, and so on.

- In addition, you can be explicit about the number of times you would like a symbol to occur by using curly braces `{min,max}`. You can specify the minimum and maximum number of times it can occur. Either one can be empty, in which case there is no minimum or maximum. Leave the comma in so OpenRefine knows whether you specified the minimum or the maximum. If you just supply a single number without a comma, the exact number of times will be matched.

- `N\d{5,8}`, matches texts that contain a code that starts with N followed by five, six, seven, or eight digits, and then a comma.

- `N\d{5,}`, matches texts that contain a code that starts with N, at least five digits, and then a comma.

- `N\d{,8}`, matches texts which contain a code that starts with N, at most eight digits, and then a comma.

- `N\d{5}`, matches texts which contain a code that starts with N, exactly five digits, and then a comma. This is equivalent to `N\d\d\d\d\d` but much more compact (especially if numbers get large).

- Needless to say, the quantifiers and braces are special symbols, so if you want to match them literally, you should escape them with a backslash. For instance, question marks can be matched with \?.

# Anchors

Sometimes, you don't only want to say how many characters to match, but also where they should be matched. This is possible with **anchors**. A caret ^ indicates that the match should happen at the beginning of a line, while a dollar sign $ indicates that the match should stop at the end of a line. (Don't confuse this with the caret inside square brackets to indicate a negation; it has a different meaning if it occurs outside of brackets.) Additionally, we can indicate that the match should begin or end at a word boundary with the anchor \b:

- ^\d matches all texts that begin with a number.

- \d$ matches all texts that end with a number.

- ^\d.*\d$ matches all texts that begin and end with a number. Read this expression as: start of the text, a number, zero or more times any character (the dot), a number, end of the text. If we would use ^\d+$ instead, we would have all texts that contain only a number (of any length).

- \b\d{3}\b searches for texts that contain at least one number of exactly three digits, since the \b anchor matches at word boundaries. If the text contains four-digit numbers but no three-digit numbers, it does not match. (If we would remove the \b anchors, it would.)

- ^\d{3}\b finds texts that start with a three-digit number.

# Choices

We have already seen a mechanism for indicating choices. Square brackets give regular expressions the possibility to choose one of the many characters: [a-z123] searches for texts with at least one lowercase letter or any of the digits 1, 2, and 3. Often, the choices are larger, as they can be several letters or words long. For this, the or operator | was introduced. It works as an OR operator between several alternatives:

- glass|wood|steel will match texts that contain glass, wood, or steel.

- \d+|many|few matches either a number, many or few.

- N\d{5},|N\d{8}, matches either five-digit or eight-digit numbers that start with an N and end with a comma, but nothing in between (so no six-digit numbers for instance).

# Groups

The only things we haven't covered so far are **groups**. If you want to use quantifiers on a group of characters instead of on a single character, you have to enclose them in parentheses ():

- While la+ matches texts that contain la, laa, laaa, and so on, the expression (la)+ finds texts that contain la, lala, lalala, and so on.

- The expression analyz|se would match texts that contain analyz and texts that contain se. This is probably not that useful. On the other hand, the expression analy(z|s)e matches both analyze and analyse. Note that in this case, this is equivalent to analy[zs]e because the choice consists of a single letter. However, this would not be the case with analyz(e|ing), which would match analyze and analyzing.

As parentheses have a special meaning, they need to be escaped as well. \( and \) match parenthesis literally.

# Overview

The following table provides an overview of the special symbols in regular expressions:

| Symbol | Meaning |
| --- | --- |
| ABC... abc... | Match the corresponding letters literally |
| 123... | Match the corresponding numbers literally |
| [xyz] | Match one of the characters inside the braces |
| [^xyz] | Match any character that is not inside the braces |
| [0-9] | Match one of the characters inside the range |
| \d | Match a digit |
| \D | Match a non-digit |
| \w | Match a letter, number, or underscore |
| \W | Match anything that is not a letter, number, or underscore |
| . | Match any character except a newline |
| \n | Match a newline |
| \. | Match an actual dot (the backslash escapes the next character) |
| ? | Match the preceding item zero or one time |
| * | Match the preceding item zero or more times |
| + | Match the preceding item one or more times |

| Symbol | Meaning |
|--------|---------|
| {3} | Match the preceding item three times |
| {3,6} | Match the preceding item three to six times |
| {3,} | Match the preceding item at least three times |
| {,6} | Match the preceding item up to six times |
| ^ | Match at the beginning of the text |
| $ | Match at the end of the text |
| \b | Match at a word boundary |
| cat\|dog\|cow | Match one of the alternatives |

# General Refine Expression Language (GREL)

The true power of regular expressions emerges if we can use them not only for finding data, but also for manipulating data. GREL enables that and a lot of other functionality as well. It is a simple language designed for easily manipulating values. It consists of a set of built-in functions as well as several variables that are available through OpenRefine. We've briefly touched upon it in several recipes and we will show you the way to build your own GREL expressions here.

## Transforming data

One place where GREL comes in handy especially is when you need to transform the values in your cells. You can either change cells in-place (by navigating to the respective column dropdown and then to **Edit cells | Transform...**) or make a new column with the transformed values (by navigating to the respective column dropdown and then to **Edit column | Add column based on this column...**). We will try some examples on the **Object Title** column here.

When you open any of the transformation dialogs, you see a first GREL expression. It is simply called value and gives back the original value of the cell. That is not really useful, but we can start from there to learn some tricks. For instance, the GREL expression "TITLE: " + value + "." adds the text TITLE: before the value and appends a dot to the end. Note that literal text must be surrounded by single or double quotes so OpenRefine doesn't confuse it with commands. You can see the preview get updated as you build the expression.

Something more useful is to change some text. For instance, we can replace the string `stone` by `stones` in each cell using `value.replace("stone", "stones")`. The `replace` function is called here on the value with the dot notation. We're telling OpenRefine to take the cell `value` and to replace all occurrences of `stone` with `stones`.

It gets all the more powerful if we combine this with regular expressions. As you can see, some of the cell values start with a number. We can remove this number by doing `value.replace(/^\d+ /, "")`. Note how the regular expression is enclosed in slashes `//`, whereas the replacement string is enclosed in double quotes `""`.

We can even go further by using groups. Not only are those used within regular expressions to treat several characters as a single unit, they also save the matched contents for later reuse. Therefore, we can replace the numbers at the start with something more meaningful. For instance: `234` becomes `Object 234:`. This is possible with the following expression: `value.replace(/^(\d+) /, "Object $1: ")`. You identify a group with a dollar sign followed by its number. The first group is called `$1`, and the special identifier `$0` is used for the result of the entire expression.

The functionality is only limited by the complexity of your expressions. A more difficult example we have noticed before is that cells in the multi-valued **Categories** column sometimes contain empty values. For instance, a value such as `"|Stones||Bones|||Buildings"` actually only contains three values, but if you split on the vertical bar, you will get seven of them (including four empty ones) because there are six divider bars. We can get rid of all these fake bars. Bars at the beginning must be removed, so we first do `value.replace(/^\|/, "")`. This looks a little more complicated than it is because the bar has to be escaped as it has a special meaning in regular expressions. To change multiple occurrences into a single one, we can do `value.replace(/\|+/, "|")`. Note how the vertical bar is escaped in the regular expression, but not in the replacement string, as it has no special meaning there.

OpenRefine has other methods than `replace`, as you can see in the useful **Help** tab of the expression editor, or in the overview at `https://github.com/OpenRefine/OpenRefine/wiki/GREL-Functions`. One example is the `split` method. When used on the **Categories** field, we can count how many different values are present in each cell as follows: `value.split("|").length()`. Here, we instruct OpenRefine to split the value whenever it encounters a vertical bar, and then uses the `length` function to count the number of resulting values. You can even build more complicated expressions such as `value.split("|").uniques().join("|")`, which, as we've seen in *Chapter 3, Advanced Data Operations*, removes duplicate values from the field.

# Creating custom facets

Now it is time to teach you something that we have been hiding for a long time: every time you create a facet, you actually execute a GREL expression. For instance, let's create a simple facet by clicking on the **Object Title** dropdown and navigating to **Facet | Customized Facets | Facet by blank**. Now click on the **change** link at the top-right of the newly created facet. OpenRefine will reveal the underlying expression just underneath the facet title and will show you a dialog box to customize the facet as shown in the following screenshot:

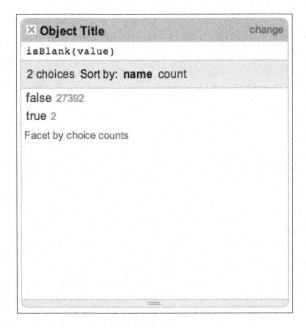

We see that the expression for a blank facet is `isBlank(value)`. Indeed, the `isBlank` function returns `true` if its value is blank and `false` if its value is not. We change this now to a different facet, for instance, if we want to know whether or not the title starts with the number 1. The expression for that would be `value.startsWith("1")`. That gives us a facet where **true** starts with 1 and **false** does not start with 1 (and **(error)** indicates that the value was empty).

> This is a great opportunity to learn about GREL. As every facet has an underlying GREL expression, you can study them to learn how they work. For instance, a **Duplicates** facet will teach you the function `facetCount`. If you're in doubt, remember that all dialogs that allow you to edit expressions also have a **Help** tab with an overview and explanation of all available functions.

If you want a facet of your own, you don't have to start with any of the pre-made facets. For instance, if we want to filter on the number of categories, we can create a custom facet by going to the **Categories** dropdown and clicking on **Facet, Custom text facet…**. Enter the expression `value.split("|").length()` and click on **OK**. You see a new **Categories** facet on the left-hand side which lets you choose the number of categories. If, like here, the output of your expression is a number, you might want to create a numeric facet instead. Follow the same steps, but navigate to **Facet | Custom numeric facet…** this time. This allows you to filter your records in a numeric way. Custom facets are a great way to explore your dataset in detail without touching your data.

# Solving problems with GREL

Finally, some knowledge of GREL comes in handy in those places where something doesn't quite work the way you expect. For instance, we saw in *Chapter 2, Analyzing and Fixing Data*, that the duplicates facet works fine on the **Registration Number** column, but not on **Record ID**. Let's see if we can fix that. Create a duplicates facet by clicking on the **Record ID** dropdown and navigating to **Facets | Customized facets | Duplicates** facet.

 Be sure to try this with the original dataset that has not been cleaned, otherwise the duplicates have already been removed.

As you might recall, OpenRefine does not find duplicates. So, let's edit the expression to update that. When we click on the **Change** link, we see the original expression:

```
facetCount(value, 'value', 'Record ID') > 1
```

The problem here is that `value` is a number and `facetCount` only works with strings. The solution is to convert `value` to a string, like this:

```
facetCount(value.toString(), 'value', 'Record ID') > 1
```

This will correctly indicate the duplicate rows in the facet.

You might be wondering: how could I ever have found this out myself? The secret is practice and exploration. The more datasets you analyze, clean, and link in OpenRefine, the better you will get at it. Also, you'll gain more and more experience with regular expressions and GREL as you gradually begin to master the basics. From that point onwards, it is a small step to the things that are increasingly complex. This book has tried to show you the direction; now it's time to go your own way.

# Index

## H

HyperText Markup Language (HTML)
code 39

## I

Interactive Data Transformation
tools (IDTs) 6

## J

Jython (Python implemented in Java) 56

## K

key collision 54
keying function 54

## L

Library of Congress Subject Headings
(LCSH) 73
Linked Data
principles 74
reconciling with 73-76
Linux
OpenRefine, installing 7

## M

Mac
OpenRefine, installing 7
matching rows
removing 41-44
memory, OpenRefine
on Linux 20
on Mac 20
on Windows 19
multi-valued cells
handling 46-48

## N

named entities, Powerhouse Museum
dataset
extracting 76-80
Named-Entity Recognition extension
URL 77

Named-Entity Recognition (NER)
extension 69
nearest neighbor 54
numeric facets 28-30

## O

OpenRefine
about 5
cell values, transforming 55
columns, manipulating 12
columns, transposing 61
columns, transposing into rows 62
data, exploring 10
data, faceting 24
data, sorting 22
data, splitting across columns 60, 61
derived columns, adding 58, 59
downloading 6
duplicate facet, detecting 34
GREL 81
installing 6
installing, on Linux 7
installing, on Mac 7
installing, on Windows 7
matching rows, removing 41
memory, allocating 19
multi-valued cells, handling 46, 47
project, creating 7, 8
project, exporting 17
project history, using 14
regular expressions 81
rows and records mode, alternating 49
rows, transposing 61
similar cells, clustering 52
simple cell transformations, using 38
supported file formats 8
text filter, applying 36
OpenRefine extensions
for Linux 71
for Mac OS X 71
for Windows 70
installing 69-71

## P

Powerhouse collection 25
Powerhouse Museum dataset

Linked Data, reconciling with  73-75
named entities, extracting  76-78
reconciliation service, adding  71
values, reconciling with Freebase  66-69
**project**
creating  7
exporting  17, 18
**project history**
accessing  15, 17

# Q

**quantifiers**
about  85
asterisk *  85
plus sign +  85
question mark ?  85

# R

**RDF  72**
**RDF extension**
downloading  71
installing  71
**reconciliation service**
adding  71
**record  49**
**records mode**
alternating, with rows mode  49-51
**regular expressions**
about  81
overview  87, 88
**regular expressions, for text patterns**
about  81
anchors  86
character classes  82
choices  86
groups  87
quantifiers  85

**Resource Description Framework.** *See* **RDF**
**row mode**
alternating, with records mode  49-51
**rows**
about  49
reordering  24
transposing  61

# S

**Semantic Web  73**
**shorthand character classes  83**
**simple cell transformations**
using  38-41
**SPARQL  72**

# T

**tab separated values (TSV)  27**
**text facets  25-28**
**text filter**
applying  36, 37
**timeline facet  29**

# U

**Unicode char-code facet  32**
**URL (Uniform Resource Locator)  65**

# W

**whitespace**
trimming  39
**Windows**
OpenRefine, installing  7

## Thank you for buying
# Using OpenRefine

# About Packt Publishing

Packt, pronounced 'packed', published its first book *"Mastering phpMyAdmin for Effective MySQL Management"* in April 2004 and subsequently continued to specialize in publishing highly focused books on specific technologies and solutions.

Our books and publications share the experiences of your fellow IT professionals in adapting and customizing today's systems, applications, and frameworks. Our solution based books give you the knowledge and power to customize the software and technologies you're using to get the job done. Packt books are more specific and less general than the IT books you have seen in the past. Our unique business model allows us to bring you more focused information, giving you more of what you need to know, and less of what you don't.

Packt is a modern, yet unique publishing company, which focuses on producing quality, cutting-edge books for communities of developers, administrators, and newbies alike. For more information, please visit our website: www.packtpub.com.

# About Packt Open Source

In 2010, Packt launched two new brands, Packt Open Source and Packt Enterprise, in order to continue its focus on specialization. This book is part of the Packt Open Source brand, home to books published on software built around Open Source licenses, and offering information to anybody from advanced developers to budding web designers. The Open Source brand also runs Packt's Open Source Royalty Scheme, by which Packt gives a royalty to each Open Source project about whose software a book is sold.

# Writing for Packt

We welcome all inquiries from people who are interested in authoring. Book proposals should be sent to author@packtpub.com. If your book idea is still at an early stage and you would like to discuss it first before writing a formal book proposal, contact us; one of our commissioning editors will get in touch with you.

We're not just looking for published authors; if you have strong technical skills but no writing experience, our experienced editors can help you develop a writing career, or simply get some additional reward for your expertise.

## Instant Weka How-to [Instant]

ISBN: 978-1-78216-386-2     Paperback: 80 pages

Implement cutting-edge data mining aspects in Weka to your applications

1. Learn something new in an Instant! A short, fast, focused guide delivering immediate results

2. A practical guide with examples and applications of programming Weka in Java

3. Start with the basics and dive deeper into the more advanced aspects of Weka

4. Learn how to include Weka's machinery in your Java application

## Instant Pentaho Data Integration Kitchen [Instant]

ISBN: 978-1-84969-690-6     Paperback: 68 pages

Explore the world of Pentaho Data Integration command-line tools which will help you use the Kitchen

1. Learn something new in an Instant! A short, fast, focused guide delivering immediate results

2. Understand how to discover the repository structure using the command line scripts

3. Learn to configure the log properly and how to gather the information that helps you investigate any kind of problem

4. Explore all the possible ways to start jobs and learn transformations without any difficulty

Please check **www.PacktPub.com** for information on our titles

## Apache Mahout Cookbook

ISBN: 978-1-84951-802-4          Paperback: 300 pages

A fast, fresh, developer-oriented dive into the world of Mahout

1.  Learn how to set up a Mahout development environment

2.  Start testing Mahout in a standalone Hadoop cluster

3.  Learn to find stock market direction using logistic regression

4.  Over 35 recipes with real-world examples to help both skilled and the non-skilled developers get the hang of the different features of Mahout

## Machine Learning with R

ISBN: 978-1-78216-214-8          Paperback: 330 pages

Learn to use R to apply powerful machine learning methods and gain insight into real-world application

1.  Harness the power of R for statistical computing and data science

2.  Use R to apply common machine learning algorithms with real-world applications

3.  Prepare, examine, and visualize data for analysis

4.  Understand how to choose between machine learning models

Please check **www.PacktPub.com** for information on our titles

CPSIA information can be obtained at www.ICGtesting.com
Printed in the USA
BVOW09s2152100316

439956BV00010B/47/P